The Stress and Mood Management Program
for Individuals with Multiple Sclerosis

✓Treatments *That Work*™

The Stress and Mood Management Program for Individuals with Multiple Sclerosis

Therapist Guide

David C. Mohr

OXFORD
UNIVERSITY PRESS

2010

OXFORD
UNIVERSITY PRESS

Oxford University Press, Inc., publishes works that further
Oxford University's objective of excellence
in research, scholarship, and education.

Oxford   New York
Auckland   Cape Town   Dar es Salaam   Hong Kong   Karachi
Kuala Lumpur   Madrid   Melbourne   Mexico City   Nairobi
New Delhi   Shanghai   Taipei   Toronto

With offices in
Argentina   Austria   Brazil   Chile   Czech Republic   France   Greece
Guatemala   Hungary   Italy   Japan   Poland   Portugal   Singapore
South Korea   Switzerland   Thailand   Turkey   Ukraine   Vietnam

Published by Oxford University Press, Inc.
198 Madison Avenue, New York, New York 10016

www.oup.com

Oxford is a registered trademark of Oxford University Press

Library of Congress Cataloging-in-Publication Data
Mohr, David C.
The stress and mood management program for individuals with multiple sclerosis : therapist
guide / David C. Mohr.
p.   ;   cm. — (TreatmentsThatWork)
Includes bibliographical references.
ISBN 978-0-19-536888-8
1. Multiple sclerosis—Psychological aspects.   2. Stress management.
3. Mood (Psychology)   I. Title.   II. Series: Treatments that work.
[DNLM: 1. Multiple Sclerosis—psychology.   2. Cognition Disorders—etiology.
3. Mood Disorders—etiology.   4. Multiple Sclerosis—complications.
5. Multiple Sclerosis—therapy.   6. Stress, Psychological—etiology. WL 360 M699s 2009]
RC377.M64 2009
616.8'34—dc22

                                                                            2009031081

9 8 7 6 5 4 3 2 1

Printed in the United States of America
on acid-free paper

About Treatments *ThatWork*™

Stunning developments have taken place in healthcare over the last several years, but many of our widely accepted interventions and strategies in mental health and behavioral medicine have been brought into question by research evidence as not only lacking benefit, but perhaps, inducing harm. Other strategies have been proven effective using the best current standards of evidence, resulting in broad-based recommendations to make these practices more available to the public. Several recent developments are behind this revolution. First, we have arrived at a much deeper understanding of pathology, both psychological and physical, which has led to the development of new, more precisely targeted interventions. Second, our research methodologies have improved substantially, such that we have reduced threats to internal and external validity, making the outcomes more directly applicable to clinical situations. Third, governments around the world and healthcare systems and policymakers have decided that the quality of care should improve, that it should be evidence-based, and that it is in public interest to ensure that this happens (Barlow, 2004; Institute of Medicine, 2001).

Of course, the major stumbling block for clinicians everywhere is the accessibility of newly developed evidence-based psychological interventions. Workshops and books can go only so far in acquainting responsible and conscientious practitioners with the latest behavioral healthcare practices and their applicability to individual patients. This new series, Treatments *ThatWork*™, is devoted to communicating these exciting new interventions to clinicians on the frontlines of practice.

The manuals and workbooks in this series contain step-by-step detailed procedures for assessing and treating specific problems and diagnoses. But this series also goes beyond the books and manuals by providing ancillary materials that will approximate the supervisory process in assisting practitioners in the implementation of these procedures in their practice.

In our emerging healthcare system, the growing consensus is that evidence-based practice offers the most responsible course of action for the mental health professional. All behavioral healthcare clinicians deeply desire to provide the best possible care for their patients. In this series, our aim is to close the dissemination and information gap and make that possible.

This therapist guide outlines a stress and mood management therapy designed to be used with patients suffering from multiple sclerosis (MS). Although almost everyone experiences stress from time to time, individuals with MS oftentimes have to deal with additional stressors. The goal of this program is to help patients improve health and well-being by teaching them skills to manage stress and depressed mood.

The program is divided into two parts, with Part I containing core chapters that outline basic cognitive-behavioral techniques such as cognitive restructuring, engaging in pleasant activities, and forming a support network. Part II consists of optional treatment modules specific to MS-related issues such as cognitive impairment, pain and fatigue, and self-injection anxiety.

Complete with lists of materials needed, session outlines, and home practice assignments, this therapist guide offers a unique and evidence-based approach to helping patients with MS manage their symptoms and improve their mental health.

David H. Barlow, Editor-in-Chief,
Treatments *That Work*™
Boston, MA

References

Barlow, D. H. (2004). Psychological treatments. *American Psychologist, 59,* 869–878.
Institute of Medicine. (2001). *Crossing the quality chasm: A new health system for the 21st century*. Washington, DC: National Academy Press.

Acknowledgments

I would like to thank my many colleagues who have helped shape my ideas and this book. In particular, I would like to acknowledge Leah Dick-Siskin, PhD, Darcy Cox, PsyD, Stacey Hart, PhD, Kelly Glaser, PhD, Jenna Duffecy, PhD, and Arne Boudewyn, PhD, who helped in writing and editing some of the sections over the years. I'd like to thank Larry Beutler, PhD, who first got me interested in researching treatments for depression, and Don Goodkin, MD, who first sparked my interest in working with people with multiple sclerosis. I am very appreciative of the support from the National Multiple Sclerosis Society and the National Institutes of Health, which have funded the research that made this book possible. And I am especially grateful to my wife, Laura, and my children, Carolina and Amalia, who patiently supported me while I was writing this book.

I also want to thank all the people with multiple sclerosis who have worked with me and my research teams over the years. Many, many people have taken part in our studies, and some people have offered comments and critiques on earlier versions of the workbook that have been incorporated into this program. I am grateful for everyone's time, effort, and generosity.

Contents

Chapter 1 | *Introductory Information for Therapists*

Purpose of the Stress and Mood Management Therapy Program

Depression, anxiety, and stress are common among patients with multiple sclerosis (MS). The stress and mood management therapy program has been developed over more than 10 years of research and clinical trials to address these problems. We initially began developing a treatment for patients who had significant symptoms of depression, both major depressive disorder and subthreshold depression. This included teaching patients skills to manage the many challenges facing them, including management of some of the symptoms of MS, social difficulties, and anxiety. After the stress and mood management therapy program was validated as a face-to-face intervention, it was tested in two trials as a telephone-administered treatment. More recently we have been testing the intervention as a stress management program. We have also developed and evaluated an intervention, included in this manual, that is aimed at treating injection anxiety, which can interfere with patients' ability to self-inject medications commonly used to control MS.

Multiple Sclerosis

MS is a chronic, often disabling disease that affects more than 400,000 people in the United States. It is believed to be a complex disease that includes an autoimmune component, in which the immune system attacks the myelin sheath around the neurons of the central nervous system, and a neurodegenerative component (Noseworthy, Lucchinetti,

Rodriguez, & Weinshenker, 2000). MS can produce a wide variety of symptoms including, but not limited to, loss of function or feeling in limbs, loss of bowel or bladder control, sexual dysfunction, blindness because of optic neuritis, loss of balance, pain, loss of cognitive functioning, and depression (Mohr & Cox, 2001; Noseworthy et al., 2000).

Usually, MS first appears between the ages of 20 and 40, but can begin earlier or later. Thus MS often affects people when they are developing careers, beginning families, and making major life decisions such as taking on a mortgage. It affects women more than twice as often as men. MS tends to be a disease of Caucasians, although it affects African Americans more frequently than Africans, and can affect other races at lower prevalence rates. Certainly genetics plays a role, but even among identical twins, concordance rates are only around 25–30%, indicating that the etiology is multifactorial. People raised in more northern latitudes have greater risk than people raised in lower latitudes, which has led to research on environmental factors such as exposure to viruses, sunlight, and a variety of other factors. Smoking is associated with an increased risk of developing MS and more rapid progression after diagnosis, but otherwise, health behaviors do not appear to have a substantial impact on the disease. The course and prognosis is very unpredictable for any individual, which creates uncertainty and anxiety.

There are several types of MS. Most people are initially diagnosed with *relapsing-remitting MS*, which is characterized by exacerbations or flares. Exacerbations are sudden increases in symptoms that appear within 24 hr. When untreated, these symptoms remit either fully or partially over a period of weeks or months, and subside much more quickly if treated with glucocorticoids (steroids). When symptoms remit only partially, the symptoms that remain are permanent. The symptoms do not progress between exacerbations. *Primary-progressive MS* is experienced by approximately 10% and is characterized by a steady worsening of symptoms without exacerbations. *Secondary-progressive MS* can be a later stage that follows relapsing-remitting MS. After a number of years of relapsing-remitting disease, symptoms begin to worsen between exacerbations, at which point a diagnosis of secondary-progressive MS is made.

Management of MS

MS is a complex chronic disease that is best managed using a multidisciplinary team. Disease-modifying medications are available for relapsing forms of the disease (relapsing-remitting and secondary-progressive). Typically these medications reduce the number of exacerbations and may slow progression. Most require injections every other day to once per week, and it is recommended that patients learn to self-inject. Depression and injection anxiety are associated with decreased adherence to these medications (Mohr, Boudewyn, Likosky, Levine, & Goodkin, 2001; Mohr et al., 1997). When injection anxiety is severe enough that the patient requires someone else to administer the injection, they are much more likely to discontinue treatment.

Apart from disease-modifying medications, treatments for MS focus principally on symptom management, which can include pharmacological treatments, physical and occupational therapies, nursing interventions, and behavioral medicine and psychological interventions.

Cognitive Impairment

The term "cognitive" in the MS world typically refers to neuropsychological symptoms rather than a term reflecting appraisal, as is common in cognitive-behavioral therapy. Therapists should be aware of this potential source of semantic confusion in communicating either with patients or with other healthcare providers. It is important for therapists working with MS patients to understand cognitive impairment as it can influence patient presentation and may require some adjustments in how care is delivered.

Neuropsychological impairment is very common, affecting up to 65% of all patients (Amato, Zipoli, & Portaccio, 2006). Impairment most commonly includes cognitive slowing, lack of attention and concentration, word-finding difficulty, and memory deficits that are characterized principally by "forgetting" rather than "amnesia." Neuropsychological impairment is somewhat independent of physical symptoms; a person can have significant physical impairment with little cognitive impairment or vice versa. Cognitive impairment is also not strongly associated with depression or mood problems, except in the most severe stages, where euphoria is sometimes present. Cognitive impairment can have a dramatic effect on quality of life, reducing a person's ability to fill a variety of work and social roles.

A patient's self-report of cognitive impairment is sometimes unreliable. Many patients without symptoms are very anxious about potential signs of cognitive impairment and may interpret normal forgetting or word-finding problems as evidence of cognitive symptoms. Indeed, symptoms of depression, anxiety, and fatigue can increase patients' perceptions of the severity of cognitive impairment. On the other hand, patients with severe impairment may underestimate the extent of their difficulties. Reports of family members tend to be more reliable. But if the patient has concerns, it may be useful to refer the patient for a neuropsychological evaluation.

An accurate understanding of the severity of cognitive impairment can be useful for several reasons. It can help patients, family members, and employers develop accurate expectations. It can help family members understand any signs of forgetfulness. It can be used to make accommodations in the patient's workplace that may allow the patient to optimize performance. If cognitive symptoms have reached a point where they significantly impair work performance, a neuropsychological evaluation can support an application for disability.

Evidence suggests that people with cognitive impairment can benefit from stress and mood management therapy. However, studies have found that greater cognitive impairment is associated with a lower likelihood that treatment gains will be sustained after the cessation of treatment (Mohr, Epstein et al., 2003). Therefore, patients with significant cognitive impairment may require a maintenance program that involves periodic check-ins.

Depression and Anxiety

A large body of evidence indicates that patients with MS are far more likely to experience depression than the general population, with lifetime prevalence rates reaching 50% and 12-month prevalence rates around 20% (Siegert & Abernethy, 2005). Although there are not as many high-quality studies examining anxiety, those that exist suggest that symptoms of anxiety are higher among patients with MS.

Stress

A large and growing literature has found that stressful life events are associated with an increased risk of MS exacerbation and of developing new MS brain lesions (Mohr, Goodkin et al., 2000; Mohr, Hart, Julian, Cox, & Pelletier, 2004). However, it remains unclear whether there is in fact a causal link. At the time of this writing, we are conducting a randomized controlled trial (RCT) to test Stress and Mood Management Therapy, with the primary outcomes being reduction of markers of MS disease activity and quality of life.

Overview of the Stress and Mood Management Therapy Program

The stress and mood management program is based on cognitive-behavioral therapy (CBT). The core chapters (3–8) of the treatment protocol utilize standard behavioral activation and cognitive restructuring techniques. It is beyond the scope of this book to provide detailed information on how to conduct CBT. We refer the interested reader to Judith Beck's *Cognitive Therapy: Basics and Beyond* (Beck, 1995).

Although many features of depression and methods of treating depression are no different for people with MS, compared to other people with depression, people with MS do confront unique difficulties related to their disease and the social role changes that occur as a result of their disease. To address these concerns, chapter 8 on social support and the optional treatment modules in Part II focus more specifically on problems that are common among MS patients. These include three classes of problems.

Social Functioning. Among patients with MS, the availability or quality of social support often declines; at the same time the need for social support increases. Chapter 8 on social support evaluates different forms of support received and provided, which can allow you to target specific areas. Module 1 on communication and assertiveness teaches skills for managing conflictual situations. In previous trials, the assertiveness interventions were used frequently and were rated as very helpful.

Anxiety. Module 3 on reducing anxiety and worry adapts cognitive restructuring to focus evaluation of threat and resources. Module 4 on relaxation can be used to provide control of physiological stress response. We also include module 7 on injection anxiety for patients whose anxiety interferes with their ability to self-inject their medications. This chapter is a condensation of an intervention program, and therefore includes approximately six sessions.

MS Symptom Management. MS symptoms can be significant stressors for many patients. Fatigue is the most common symptom, cited by 78% of patients (Freal, Kraft, & Coryell, 1984). Module 2 on fatigue and energy conservation teaches skills that can reduce the impact of fatigue on functioning. Pain is experienced by nearly 50% of MS patients (O'Connor, Schwid, Herrmann, Markman, & Dworkin, 2008) and is addressed in module 5 on pain management. Cognitive impairment is also common, as noted previously, and is addressed in module 6 on planning and organization. This module may also help people who are experiencing stress because of poor organizational skills.

Although pharmacological treatments and rehabilitation interventions for these symptoms are available, they are often only moderately effective. The strategies outlined in these modules teach methods of minimizing the impact of these symptoms on functioning and quality of life. We should note that MS patients experience many more symptoms (e.g. mobility impairments, spasticity, urinary and bowel dysfunction). The methods used in this book may also be applicable to managing the impact of some of these symptoms on quality of life.

Therapy Structure

This treatment has been tested in both 8-week and 16-week formats. For most patients, 16 weeks is far more preferable, as improvements in key symptoms continue to improve throughout the therapy. Sessions are usually 45–50 min. As described in chapter 2, a thorough assessment of the patient's functioning is recommended. The need for assessment and rapid initiation of treatment can be handled in one of two ways. In one trial, we had two sessions in the first week. In another, we extended the first session to 90 min. Both have been acceptable to patients. When completing therapy, it is recommended that you begin spacing sessions out to once every 2–3 weeks to allow the patient to begin practicing skills for maintenance of gains.

Pace of Therapy

Within the sessions, it is usually best to spend the bulk of the time reviewing homework. After all, homework is where patients implement the changes in their lives, and ultimately the changes in their lives are what are important. Many (but not all) of the chapters and modules are written so that they can be delivered in one session. But there is no need to try to push patients through at that rate. Take as long as needed to help patients grasp the concepts and do the homework correctly. It is better that they learn a few things well, than race through and be only superficially exposed to many chapters and modules.

Use of the Workbook

In RCTs testing the stress and mood management program among people with MS, both the therapist and the patient worked principally from the patient workbook. The workbook is intended to provide a clear description of the evidence-based intervention concepts and procedures for the patient, to help ensure that the patient understands the concepts. The workbook is also intended as a resource for patients after the completion of treatment to support maintenance of gains. More specific to patients with cognitive impairment, the workbook can serve as a reminder to reinforce the learning that occurs in the session. Finally, the workbook can support telephone-administered treatments, as will be discussed later on in the chapter.

We recommend that the patient read ahead, when appropriate. But if the patient does not comply with reading assignments, it is not critical (in contrast to the other homework assignments, which are critical). We strongly urge you, as the therapist, to read the entire therapist manual and the workbook before embarking on the treatment. It is important to keep a copy of the workbook in your clinic office, in case the patient forgets hers. Use the workbook when practicing filling out the forms for the exercises. Many therapists and patients also find it useful to have the workbook open to the relevant pages when the concepts are being presented to the patient.

Development and Evidence Base

We began investigating treatments for depression in MS, because depression is common and little was known about the efficacy of treatments. Based upon the clinical experience gained through treating patients at the University of California, San Francisco's (UCSF) MS Center, we developed our first patient workbook designed to treat depressive symptoms. This was initially based on the work of Dolores Gallagher-Thompson and Larry Thompson (Gallagher-Thompson, Hanley-Peterson, & Thompson, 1990; Thompson, Gallagher, and Breckenridge, 1987.) At that time there were two other commonly recommended treatments for depression: antidepressant medication and group therapy. Our first study compared three forms of 16-week treatments that had been recommended for MS patients: (1) an individual CBT that was a first version of the stress and mood management therapy program; (2) supportive expressive group therapy (Spiegel & Classen, 2000); and (3) the antidepressant sertraline. We selected supportive expressive group therapy because a validated treatment manual was available. We were also able to collaborate with the Spiegel lab to ensure therapist fidelity in treatment delivery. We selected sertraline as the antidepressant because a survey of neurologists at a national MS meeting identified sertraline as the most commonly prescribed antidepressant at that time. We initially did not hypothesize that there would be differences between the treatments (rather we had hypotheses predicting which patients would fare best in which treatments). The individual CBT and sertraline produced equivalently beneficial reductions in depression. However, to our surprise, the supportive expressive group therapy produced no significant benefit (Mohr, Boudewyn, Goodkin, Bostrom, & Epstein, 2001). This was our first finding that it actually may matter which treatment modality is used with MS patients.

Although MS patients were generally very interested in receiving treatment, many had barriers that prevented them from coming into the clinic on a weekly basis. These barriers included MS symptoms, transportation problems, or living too far away. Accordingly, we embarked on a set of trials to examine telephone-administered psychotherapy for depression in MS. The first trial, conducted through neurology clinics in the Northern California Kaiser Permanente Group, compared 8 weekly 50-min sessions of telephone-administered stress and mood management therapy (including the patient workbook) to the usual care provided by neurologists. We recruited patients with moderate levels of depressed mood who were initiating treatment on an injectable MS disease-modifying medication. We found significant improvements in depressive symptoms, as well as increased adherence to MS disease-modifying medications (Mohr, Likosky et al., 2000). A second larger study compared the telephone-administered stress and mood management therapy to a telephone-administered version of a manualized and validated treatment called Supportive Emotion-Focused Therapy (SEFT) (Greenberg, Rice, & Elliott, 1993) for the treatment of depressive symptoms among patients with MS. All patients received 16 weekly sessions delivered by doctoral-level psychologists. The telephone-administered stress and mood management therapy produced significantly greater reductions in depression as measured by diagnosis of major depressive disorder and on severity of depressive symptoms rated by an independent, blinded evaluator (Mohr, Hart et al., 2005). It is important to note that in face-to-face comparisons among medically healthy depressed patients, SEFT and CBT have been shown to be equivalent (Watson, Gordon, Stermac, Kalogerakos, & Steckley, 2003). This was the second time we found stress and mood management therapy to be superior to a non-CBT-based validated treatment. We suspect that part of the reason for the superiority of our treatment is that it provides specific skills training for managing the difficulties and stresses experienced by patients with MS.

Our research has also found that stress and mood management therapy produces a number of additional important benefits. Patients who receive this treatment show significant improvements in social functioning (Mohr, Classen, & Barrera, 2004).

There were significant improvements in disability as rated by blinded evaluators and in self-ratings of the severity of symptoms such as fatigue (Mohr, Hart, & Goldberg, 2003; Mohr, Hart, & Vella, 2007). Patients demonstrated improvements on a variety of markers of positive functioning, including positive affect, benefit finding (finding benefits in having MS such as valuing relationships or increased spirituality), and optimism (S. L. Hart, Vella, & Mohr, 2008; Mohr, Hart et al., 2005). Finally, overall quality of life has also shown significant improvement (Hart, Fonareva, Merluzzi, & Mohr, 2005).

Self-Injection Anxiety

The studies just described did not include the module on self-injection anxiety (module 7). We developed the Self-Injection Anxiety Therapy (SIAT) when the first injectable medications became available for MS. We noticed that substantial numbers of patients were unable to self-inject, and began working with these patients at the UCSF MS Center to help them overcome their anxieties and phobias. Once we developed a protocol and a patient workbook, we tested the intervention in a small feasibility trial of MS patients who were prescribed injectable medications but were unable to self-inject because of anxiety. By the end of the 6-week treatment, seven out of eight patients were able to successfully self-inject. The eighth patient was able to self-inject with an additional seventh session (Mohr, Cox, Epstein, & Boudewyn, 2002).

In a second RCT we taught nurses to administer the self-injection therapy. Eight out of eleven patients completing the treatment were able to self-inject, compared to 3 out of 12 patients completing a relaxation therapy (Mohr, Cox, & Merluzzi, 2005). Many of the patients who learned to self-inject in these trials had substantial difficulties, including diagnosable injection phobias and vasovagal responses (e.g. fainting and nausea) to the sight of needles. Thus, although these trials are small, they provide evidence that the self-injection module can be effective in teaching patients to self-inject their medications.

MS is a complex disease that involves many healthcare specialists. Patients are best served when their providers work collaboratively. The healthcare team is organized through the patient's physician. Usually this is the primary care physician; however, for many MS patients the neurologist becomes a central point of organization. Physical and occupational therapists communicate with the physician. Medical specialties such as radiology communicate with the patient's physician. Mental health professionals should as well.

Why is it important that you be part of the team? As the patient's therapist, you have an important role to play. For example, more than 80% of antidepressants are prescribed by primary care physicians and nonmental health physicians. We have found that nearly all neurologists prescribe only the minimal dose of antidepressants for depressed MS patients, which is far less than is required for patients to obtain symptom remission (Mohr, Hart, Fonareva, & Tasch, 2006). If a collaborative relationship is developed with the patient's physician, we have found that most physicians welcome recommendations for psychotropic medications or medication adjustments. Physicians may also have information that is useful for you. And they may want your help with other behavioral medicine problems (e.g. compliance with medications, assessment and management of neuropsychological problems).

To maintain a collaborative relationship, the following steps are recommended:

- Obtain the patient's consent and release of information from the patient to communicate with the physician(s).

- Inform the physician(s) that you have seen the patient (and thank them if they made the referral). Provide your diagnosis of the patient, a problem list or complicating factors (e.g. suicidality, cognitive impairment, extraordinary life circumstances), and a treatment plan (e.g. an evidence-based cognitive-behavioral therapy). You can provide this information via letter or any other method the clinic accepts.

- Follow up with updates to the physician(s) on a regular basis (every month or two). Provide information on status (diagnosis, symptoms, and problem list) and update your treatment plan.

- If you have questions about the medical treatment, ask the physician.

- If you have recommendations for treatment, for example about psychotropic medications, let the physician(s) know.

- Keep your communications very brief—a paragraph or two, and/or a few bullet points at most. Physicians do not want detailed notes. They want brief, broad, easily scannable information.

This type of simple contact takes very little time and can substantially improve the care that patients receive.

Telephone-Administered Stress and Mood Management Therapy

A growing literature indicates that approximately two-thirds of depressed patients want psychotherapy as part of their treatment plan. But 75% of depressed patients have one or more barriers that make it impossible to attend regularly scheduled face-to-face psychotherapy sessions. Although cost is certainly a barrier, many other barriers, such as time constraints, transportation problems, and physical disability, also prevent access to care (Mohr, Hart, Howard et al., 2006).

The telephone has proven to be an effective method of delivering care and may well overcome many of these barriers. Compared to more than 50% of patients who drop out or do not complete face-to-face psychological treatments, a recent meta-analysis found that only approximately 7.6% drop out of telephone psychotherapy (Mohr, Vella, Hart, Heckman, & Simon, 2008). This suggests that telephone-administered treatments may help overcome many barriers to care.

Procedures Specific to Telephone-Administered Treatment

Psychotherapy can be provided over the phone in a fashion very similar to face-to-face delivery. We've found that therapists, when first beginning to use the telephone, are concerned that the lack of visual cues may diminish their ability to deliver quality care. But in most circumstances, therapists quickly find that they can establish good therapeutic bonds over the telephone (Beckner, Vella, Howard, & Mohr, 2007). Much of the nonverbal information patients provide can be gleaned from voice quality (Mohr, Shoham-Salomon, Engle, & Beutler, 1991). The exception to this is when patients are silent; in these cases it is difficult to discern whether the silence is due to rising anxiety or is simply a contemplative moment. In such instances the therapist can verbally inquire what the patient is experiencing.

There are a few procedural issues that are unique to telephone therapy. Because the therapist has less control over the environment in which the patient is receiving the therapy, it is important to review the following items with the patient:

- Be sure the patient is safe. Never conduct sessions while the patient is driving.

- Use a telephone with a clear connection.

- Ensure privacy. Ask that the patient use a private room, where she will not be overheard.

- Ensure that the patient is not interrupted. Ask the patient to let everyone in the house know she will not be available while working with you. If the patient has small children, see if she can arrange to have someone watch them.

- Be sure the room is free of distractions. Have the patient turn off radios, televisions, computers, and any other potential disturbances.

- If the patient has call waiting, ask that she not answer incoming calls during your session unless it is absolutely necessary.

- Ask patients to take care of personal needs before the appointment, such as using the bathroom, having a glass of water, or tissues available.

- Ask the patient to have her workbook with her, along with a pen or pencil.

- Suggest that the patient use headphones so that she can take notes.

- Ask that the patient be available for the call at the appointment time, and be sure to allot the full 45–50 min as patients sometimes take a more casual approach to scheduling when sessions are conducted over the telephone.

Be aware that it is not always feasible for patients to comply with all of these requests. Telephone-administered psychotherapy is often required precisely because patients have other responsibilities that would interfere with face-to-face treatment. When patients are unable to create the ideal environment for therapy, it is important to discuss these issues with the patient and to come to an agreement about how to manage the treatment.

It is important to note for practitioners in the United States that at the time of this writing treatment is legally considered to occur where the patient is, and not where the therapist is. Therefore, when providing telephone-administered treatment, the therapist must be licensed in the state where the patient is at the time treatment is delivered. Also, at the time of this writing, insurance in the United States generally does not cover telephone-administered services. However, this may be changing. The US Centers for Medicare and Medicaid Services have proposed health and behavior billing codes for telephone-administered services for psychologists under some conditions.

Safety with Telephone-Administered Treatment

The most common emergent situation among patients with MS is suicidality. Standard procedures can be employed with patients treated remotely. A call to emergency services (911 in the United States) should be able to connect you to local emergency services, which can be asked to go to the patient's location to conduct a safety check. Be sure you know where the patient lives.

The National Multiple Sclerosis Society (NMSS) is a superb source of information for patients and clinicians. Their Web site at www.nmss.org contains a wealth of information about the disease, the types of problems faced by patients, and treatments. In addition, local NMSS chapters can often provide resources for patients, including referrals for a variety of medical, legal, and social service services. Many local chapters also organize programs for MS patients that can range from educational programs to supportive services.

Chapter 2 | *Assessment*

Introduction

A thorough assessment of the patient's functioning is critical to meeting the needs of the patient. A standard intake evaluation should be conducted. It is beyond the scope of this chapter to describe the standard components of such an evaluation. The purpose of this chapter is to present MS-specific information that should be included in the evaluation.

Mental Health

A diagnostic interview should be performed that includes all of the major diagnostic categories. Patients with MS—even if they are coming to you for a specific MS-related problem—are not immune to other mental health problems. It is useful to determine the severity of the patient's emotional symptoms. As noted in chapter 1, mood and anxiety disorders are common. Anger and irritability are also common and can be disruptive to the patient's social functioning.

Evaluate the patient's history of mental healthcare, including medications, therapies, and hospitalizations. With respect to previous therapy, it is useful to understand what occurred as part of that therapy and how satisfied the patient was with the process and outcome of therapy. If there is any history of dissatisfaction, it is important to ascertain what specifically was unhelpful or disagreeable, and talk with the patient how to ensure that these problems do not occur with you. Regular assessment of potential problems over the course of treatment is advisable to prevent such difficulties from interfering with your treatment of the patient.

Suicidality

A careful assessment of suicidality should be conducted with all new patients. Suicidal ideation is common among MS patients and rates of suicide are far higher than among the general public. A suicide evaluation should address the following:

- Does the patient have suicidal ideation? Although suicidal ideation is common among patients with MS, it is not normative and should be taken seriously.

- Evaluate the lethality of any plan.

- Evaluate the feasibility of any plan.

- Evaluate the presence and history of suicidal behavior. Does the patient have a history of suicide attempts? Is he currently engaging in behaviors that are dangerous (e.g. self-mutilation)?

- Why does the patient want to kill himself? Is it related to depression and hopelessness? Or is it a plan related to fear of future disability—a method managing anxiety about an uncertain but threatening future.

- What events would bring the patient to the point of acting on the impulses? How likely are these events to occur?

- What keeps the patient from acting on the impulses? For example, is the patient concerned about the effect suicide would have on children or loved ones? Does the patient have religious beliefs that prevent him from killing himself?

- How has the patient coped with suicidal impulses in the past?

- Identify factors that might impair the patient's judgment, such as alcohol or substance use, or judgment and reasoning deficits associated with cognitive impairment.

Health

A thorough medical history should be conducted that includes both MS and other medical problems. Patients with MS are just as likely as any other patient to have other non-MS health problems. These should be evaluated just as you would in any intake evaluation. The following sections describe the components of the health evaluation that are specific to MS.

Date of MS Diagnosis

When was the MS diagnosis made? Patients who have been recently diagnosed (e.g. within the past few years) often experience anxiety and worry about an uncertain future. But given the progressive nature of the disease, adjustment to new symptoms or disabilities can be a periodic issue.

Course of MS

The course may vary greatly from one patient to another. Some patients may have a fairly stable disease, with little deterioration over time, whereas others may have more aggressive disease marked by frequent exacerbations and/or more rapid decline.

Evaluation of MS Symptoms

In assessing MS symptoms, evaluate the presence of the symptom, the severity, and the degree to which it interferes with the patient's ability to perform social roles, including work, social life, and family roles. The more common symptoms and some of the treatments are listed here. If you detect untreated symptoms, you should take an active role in encouraging the patient to obtain appropriate treatment.

Fatigue

Fatigue should be evaluated as part of the intake interview. A more thorough evaluation of fatigue can be conducted as part of module 2 on fatigue and energy conservation. Several medications are available that can significantly reduce fatigue severity for many patients, and various physical therapy and compensatory strategies, including those discussed in this manual, can be helpful.

Cognitive Impairment

Cognitive impairment is difficult to evaluate accurately without a thorough neuropsychological assessment. If patients have had such testing, it is useful to request a copy of the report. Although it is important to ask the patient about his cognitive symptoms, patient self-report of cognitive impairment is not always reliable. In particular, depression, anxiety, and fatigue can increase self-reported severity. Commonly used objective screening instruments such as the Mini Mental Status Exam do not accurately assess MS-related cognitive impairment. The Paced Auditory Serial-Addition Test (Gronwall, 1997) is a brief reasonable screening instrument for cognitive impairment in MS, but requires purchase of a CD. Evaluation of cognitive changes by family members tends to be more accurate than patient self-report. In the absence of objective testing, treatment can continue, and it is useful simply to be alert to potential interference from cognitive symptoms. If cognitive impairment appears to interfere with treatment, a neuropsychological evaluation and consultation should be considered.

Pain

Pain should be evaluated, given that the program includes a module on pain management. Various pharmacological treatments are also available that are helpful in reducing pain severity.

Urinary Incontinence

Urinary incontinence is common and can have several different etiologies. Patients with urinary incontinence sometimes restrict their fluid intake as a coping strategy. This is potentially problematic as it can lead to urinary tract infections and other health problems. Effective pharmacological treatments are available, although patients sometimes complain of the side effects. Various catheters can also be used.

Bowel Incontinence

Although rare, bowel incontinence can cause patients to significantly restrict their social activities, as patients can find soiling accidents shameful or humiliating. Constipation is far more common. Bowel problems are typically managed with dietary management and sometimes medications.

Spasticity and Tremors

Spasticity and tremors can impair functioning and restrict social functioning and are typically managed both with medications and, for spasticity, with stretching exercises.

Sleep Disorders

Sleep problems are common in MS and can be caused or aggravated by pain, urinary urgency, spasticity and tremors, depression and anxiety, as well as other symptoms. The symptoms that may be interfering with sleep can be treated; in addition, a cognitive-behavioral treatment for insomnia may be helpful. You may want to refer the patient to *Overcoming Insomnia, Workbook* (Edinger & Carney, 2008).

Weakness

Weakness, particularly in the legs, is common and is typically treated with physical therapy and with the use of adaptive equipment such as braces.

Sexual Dysfunction

Sexual problems are common and can be aggravated by many of the medications used to manage other MS symptoms. Women experiencing sexual dysfunction most frequently experience numbness in the genital area, diminished orgasmic response, unpleasant sensations, and diminished vaginal lubrication. The use of water-soluble lubricants may be an essential aid in genital stimulation and sexual arousal. Men commonly report impaired genital sensation, delayed ejaculation, decreased force of ejaculation, and/or an inability to achieve and maintain an erection. Medications such as sildenafil (Viagra®) can be helpful. Couples therapy is often a critical component of treatment for sexual dysfunction.

MS Exacerbation History

People with relapsing-remitting MS most commonly have an exacerbation every year or two, although, like everything else in MS, this can vary substantially from patient to patient. Exacerbations can cause significant disruption in a person's life, including lost time at work. Exacerbations are typically accompanied by significant distress, which may be the result of inflammatory processes, rather than psychosocial reactions. Exacerbations are typically treated with glucocorticoids (steroids) administered in large doses through infusions or orally. Some patients find the side effects of these drugs unpleasant, and sometimes stop going to their physician for exacerbations, since there is little else that can be provided. You should be aware that patient reports of exacerbations frequently do not correspond to neurologist-confirmed exacerbations, and this is sometimes a source of frustration for patients. This does not mean that patient reports are not important. Multiple factors can produce symptoms that seem like exacerbations, including infection (e.g. urinary tract infections), heat, waxing and waning of symptoms, to name a few. Whether confirmed or unconfirmed by neurologists, the distress that these symptoms cause is real.

Medication Adherence

Evaluate the patient's adherence to any prescribed medications. Many of the medications used to manage MS symptoms have unpleasant side effects that can cause patients to limit the use of these medications. Evaluate the patient's use of disease-modifying medications.

The most commonly used medications are beta-interferons (Avonex®, Betaseron®, or Rebif®) and glatiramer acetate (Copaxone®), which are all injectables. Ask if the patient self-injects or if he has someone else to administer the injection. Self-injection is generally associated with greater adherence. If patients are physically capable of self-injecting, but are unable to because of anxiety or phobia, module 7—Self-Injection Anxiety Counseling—may be particularly useful.

Medical Care

Ask about the patient's current medical care team. As noted in chapter 1, it is important to get the names of the patient's neurologist and primary care physician. If the patient agrees, keep them informed about your treatment of the patient. Inquire as to the use of other medical treatments such as physical or occupational therapy. Ask about the patient's satisfaction with his current care and current care providers. Helping patients manage their healthcare and preventing psychological symptoms from interfering with their healthcare should be part of this therapy.

Social Functioning

The components of an evaluation of social functioning include current relationships with family and friends, current work functioning, and history of relationships and work functioning. Even though a more detailed evaluation of social supports is conducted as part of chapter 8, a preliminary evaluation should be conducted upon intake. MS is a disease that affects not only the patient, but also family members and loved ones. As patients experience more symptoms and need more help, they often have dwindling support networks, which can create strains on those who remain. Evaluate both the number of people and the quality of the social network. Ask how MS may have affected those relationships. Evaluation of relationship history can help distinguish the degree to which current social problems may be a consequence of current life circumstances and to what extent long-standing interpersonal and social skills deficits contribute to problems.

MS can have a significant impact on a person's ability to perform work roles. For patients who are working, difficulties in the performance of work activities should be carefully evaluated. Often accommodations can be made in the workplace to help optimize patients' performance. However, MS can impact the work environment in other ways. Frequently there are concerns about possible discrimination and how superiors will view the patient's MS. Some patients are hesitant to request accommodations for fear of social repercussions.

It is useful to ask whom the patient has told that he has MS and whom he has not told. Many patients are fairly open about their diagnosis, but many also have groups of people whom they do not tell. It can be useful to understand why they are hesitant to tell some people. Sometimes the hesitancy is a reflection of shame or anxiety about the reactions of others. Other times it may be an adaptive response to very real concerns about stigma and discrimination. However, even when concerns about stigma and discrimination in the workplace are valid, failure to disclose the MS diagnosis to superiors can leave the patient more vulnerable, as protections afforded under the Americans with Disabilities Act are only in force if the employer knows about the disability.

Developmental Milestones

As noted in chapter 1, MS typically affects people in the prime of life, when they are developing intimate relationships, establishing families, making decisions about having children, making major financial decisions such as whether to buy a house, and choosing or developing careers. The uncertainty that accompanies MS can have a significant impact on a person's ability to manage these developmental processes and decisions. A discussion of how the patient is managing these areas of his life is an important part of an initial evaluation.

Issues of MS

The following are common issues that cause distress among patients with MS. This framework was borrowed from the work of Irene Pollin

(Pollin, 1995). The author has found that these issues are often recurring themes running through many of the problems faced by patients. Asking specifically about each of these issues elicits considerable information that can be clinically useful. The author has also found that this expresses to patients that you understand the difficulties that he faces. Not all patients will endorse all issues. But most will find at least a few relevant.

Fears of Loss of Control

Some people with MS experience a sense of loss of control over their body, thoughts, or feelings. For example, being diagnosed or the sudden appearance of a new symptom may contribute to a feeling of a loss of control over one's body or destiny. Sometimes, in reaction, people experience racing thoughts or constant worries that they cannot control and/or a loss of control over feelings such as overwhelming sadness, fear, or anger. The perception of having little control can be aggravated by the occurrence of an exacerbation, new symptoms, the unpredictability of the disease and its course, having to rely on others, fears about the future, and many other things. These feelings of little control can reemerge at different times in one's life because of MS exacerbations or other life events.

Overwhelming feelings of loss of control can lead to maladaptive attempts to gain back control or alleviate the anxiety caused by the loss of control. Such reactions may include leaving a job prematurely, seeking potentially dangerous or expensive "alternative" treatments, or giving up important responsibilities. It is also common that those who feel like they are losing control end up trying to gain back their sense of control by controlling others.

Fears of Dependency

Many people with MS fear that future physical decline will result in their becoming dependent on others emotionally, physically, medically, and/or financially. Concerns about dependency encompass not only worries about the loss of personal independence, but also worries about burdening others. For example, soon after diagnosis, people often fear that they will eventually require a wheelchair for mobility and will have to rely on others. The thought of having to rely on others can be particularly worrisome for people who place a high value on their independence. It is not uncommon for people with such concerns to fight against the fears of losing independence by ignoring bodily signals to slow down or discounting medical recommendations for assistance. Another way people fight becoming dependent is by withdrawing from their family and friends on whom they might depend.

At the same time, people sometimes also like the idea of others taking care of them. Often this approach leads to people giving up responsibilities and withdrawing from active engagement in life. But giving up responsibilities can leave people feeling empty, hopeless, or useless. Managing issues and fears around dependence usually requires awareness of one's thoughts and feelings around dependence, and finding a balance.

Self-Image

Like many chronic illnesses, MS challenges one's self-image. Self-image consists of the beliefs and values one has about one's self, abilities and capacities, social roles, and body image. To the degree that MS affects any of these areas, a patient may experience changes in self-image. For example, many people without chronic illnesses maintain a self-image that includes being healthy or strong. Having a chronic illness can change that. For some it may just be a general sense of vulnerability. For others, there may be real losses. Someone who values his athleticism and sees himself as "strong" and "energetic" might begin to feel weak and ineffectual if MS-related fatigue or other symptoms interfere with athletics. For a man who believes playing sports with his son is central to his role as a father, not being able to do so might cause feelings of being a failure as a father. For a woman who prides herself on her independence, tenaciousness, and success at work, having difficulty in performing her job because of MS symptoms may lead her to question her value as a person.

Stigma

MS may also impact how others view the patient. Over time, society has become more tolerant of differences. But people who are different, including those who are chronically ill or disabled, may still be stigmatized. Stigmatization can include various responses, including avoidance, fear, discrimination, hostility, condescension, disgust, or simple curiosity. There are very concrete ways that society stigmatizes people with chronic illnesses, including job or health insurance discrimination. Even people who do not have visible symptoms (or are just developing visible symptoms) often fear or worry about the stigma that they might encounter later. These anticipatory worries about stigma can be very unsettling.

Issues of stigma are sometimes hard to sort out and can be confused with self-image. While others sometimes stigmatize individuals with chronic illnesses or disabilities, the patient's own feelings about chronic illness and disability can also contribute to a perception of stigma. That is, the patient may attribute the negative thoughts or attitudes that he has about chronic illness or disability to others, and imagine that others have the same thoughts about him. For example, a person who once may have had disparaging thoughts about someone with a chronic illness may now worry that others will have similar thoughts about him.

This is not to minimize stigma, which is real and ubiquitous. But it is important to evaluate the extent to which perceptions of stigma may be related to self-image, or internalized stigma, which would suggest different approaches to coping compared to managing stigma in the social environment.

Social Isolation and Fear of Abandonment

The fear of being alone can be one of the most profound fears a patient can have. People with serious or chronic illnesses may fear that their loved ones and families will abandon them. Single patients with MS often fear they will never find a partner. Related to this, many people with chronic illnesses are isolated. Isolation can be physical, social, and emotional. Physically, symptoms can make it harder to remain socially active. Emotionally, patients often believe that nobody really understands what they are experiencing, which leads to a sense of isolation and alienation.

Shame

Shame is a feeling that arises when a person perceives that a personal shortcoming has been exposed publicly. Chronic illnesses such as MS can increase the risk that people feel ashamed. Sometimes symptoms interfere with being able to meet people's expectations. For example, fatigue may interfere with being able to meet a social obligation. People with MS commonly believe (perhaps rightly so) that others will not understand the fatigue they experience, leaving them unable to explain their difficulty in meeting the social obligation. Other times the symptom itself may cause embarrassment. For example, walking or balance difficulties are sometimes perceived by others as a sign of intoxication. And many people with bowel or bladder problems have had embarrassing accidents in public. Shame is a potentially damaging feeling because it often provokes social withdrawal and sometimes self-criticism.

Integration of the Intake Assessment

A thorough assessment can take time. The author has found this usually takes most of the first meeting and sometimes some of the second session. As noted in chapter 1, to begin treatment promptly, it is recommended that you conduct two sessions in the first week, or allow 90 min for the first session. When patients show severe levels of depression, two sessions per week is advisable for the first 2–4 weeks.

Core Treatment Chapters

Chapter 3 | *Introduction to Stress and Mood Management*

(Corresponds to chapter 1 of the workbook)

Materials Needed

- Copy of patient workbook

Outline

- Set the agenda
- Rate the patient's stress/distress level
- Introduce the stress management program for MS
- Discuss the importance of the collaborative relationship in therapy and clarify therapist and patient roles
- Introduce rationale for stress management
- Discuss where distress and mood problems come from
- Explain what stress is and where it comes from
- Introduce patient to the stress and mood management model
- Summarize the session
- Assign homework

Setting the Agenda

Set an agenda for today's session and all subsequent sessions with the patient. It is very important to begin setting an agenda from the very first session. Write the agenda down. Read the list back to the patient when you and the patient have agreed on what you are going to cover. Explain to the patient that together you will be setting the agenda in order to make the best use of the available time. For example, you may say something like the following:

> *I'd like to begin our meeting by going over what it is that we are going to talk about today. I'll be asking you some questions about how you are feeling and what brings you in to see me. We'll also talk a little bit about where the problems you are having might come from, how this treatment can help, and what you will need to do as part of this treatment. Is there anything you would like to add to this list, so I can be sure we have time to get to it?*

An agenda helps keep the session on target, and gives the therapist a way to intervene if the patient begins rambling or introducing new topics. For example, if the patient begins going off on a tangent, an agenda will allow you to say something like "I notice that this is not a topic that is on the agenda. Is it something you want to add to the agenda, or do you want to hold onto it and discuss it at our next meeting?" This will allow you to make a decision whether to talk about this and drop something else from the agenda, or postpone this topic.

Rating Stress Levels

Have the patient rate his stress or distress level on a 1–10 scale, with 1 signifying a total lack of stress and 10 signifying the highest level of stress possible. Make a note of the patient's ratings in your records. At subsequent sessions this will allow you to reinforce improvements and ask about what contributed to change.

Initial Assessment

Ask what brings the patient in to see you. Get some information about:

- Sources of stress and distress

- Aggravating factors

- Coping effectiveness (what has the patient done that can improve this or similar situations)

- Social network and supports (who the patient's friends and family are, the quality of the relationships, and satisfaction with support). Chapter 8 examines social support in more detail.

- Medical factors, including MS symptoms, other illnesses, and medications. Ask specifically about covert MS symptoms including cognitive (neuropsychological) impairment, fatigue, pain, bowel and bladder problems. Evaluate the impact of these symptoms on social role functioning (work, family duties, social engagement, etc.). Chapters 1 and 2 provide more detail about MS-specific problems.

- Previous mental/behavioral health problems and treatment. Ask specifically about depression, anxiety, and suicidal ideation.

This assessment may extend into the second session. It is OK to halt the evaluation to discuss the topics in the sections that follow. It is important to be sure the patient understands the goals of the program, expectations for the patient, and the treatment model, as well as to leave with a homework assignment.

Introduction to the Stress and Mood Management Program for MS

Goals for the Program

Present the goals of the program to the patient:

- Enable the patient to improve his quality of life

- Improve mood and enjoyment

Explain that this program will focus primarily on teaching stress management skills, such as coping and social support enhancement. The program will help the patient implement these skills in his everyday life. During the first couple of weeks of the program, you should talk with the patient about how MS has affected him. Tell the patient that as he is the best judge of what the main sources of stress are in his life, he will largely decide how much this program focuses on stress related to MS, and how much it will focus on other problems or issues.

Structure of the Program

Describe the structure of the program to the patient. Typically, treatment takes 16 sessions of 45–50 min over a period of approximately 18 weeks. In practice, the number of sessions of course will vary depending on the needs of the patient. If a patient shows significant symptoms of depression, it is advisable to have two sessions per week for the first 1–4 weeks. After this first meeting, each subsequent meeting consists of the following:

1. Check-in. The patient rates his overall level of stress or distress. This is so that you and the patient can keep track of the patient's progress.

2. Setting an agenda for the session. This is a way to make sure the patient can bring up issues he wants to talk about, as well as allow time for the presentation of new material.

3. Reviewing homework.

4. Discussing new material as well as anything the patient would like to bring up.

5. Summarizing the meeting and discussing homework for the coming week.

Some patients may ask, "Why is this therapy expected to be 18 weeks?" You may want to answer with something like the following:

We know that 18 weeks is a long time, but making changes in how you manage stress is difficult. The first 14 weeks are focused on teaching you skills and helping you begin making changes in your life that will reduce stress and improve your quality of life. The last two meetings are spread out, approximately 2 weeks apart. This is to help you integrate the new skills into your life and to help you maintain the changes you have made for the long term.

The *collaborative relationship* is a core feature of any cognitive-behavioral therapy. This means that the patient should be included in decision making and should be encouraged to take responsibility for his treatment. It also means that you, as the therapist, should be actively engaged in making your expertise available to the patient. Patients are encouraged to be good consumers of mental healthcare. As such, we encourage patients to ask therapists any questions about the process of therapy and the therapist's expertise. By encouraging such discussion and openly answering appropriate questions, therapists support patient empowerment in their health and mental healthcare.

To facilitate an understanding of the collaborative relationship, discuss the following roles and responsibilities.

The Role of the Therapist

Your role as a therapist is to:

- provide expertise that will help the patient develop new skills and understanding to better manage his problems.

- be trained, knowledgeable, and proficient in CBT. You should also have experience working with people with chronic illnesses. It is important to be straightforward about what your experience is and/or is not. To the extent that you do not have experience with the specific problems facing the patient, being clear will provide a more solid basis for a collaborative relationship. The patient should also help you understand his experience.

- seek to understand the patient's experience.

- obtain and provide feedback as doing so is a core principle of the collaborative relationship. Obtain feedback on the patient's understanding of the material covered and correct any misunderstandings. Assess the patient's satisfaction and ask if there is anything he would like done differently. You should also provide feedback that is supportive, and also honest.

- include the patient in the decisions such as setting goals for therapy, conducting sessions, and choosing homework assignments. You should also provide your input.

- help the patient learn new skills to manage problems.

- explain all agreements of treatment, including fees, how much advance notice is required for cancelling sessions, the need to be on time for appointments, etc. We recommend these be provided in a written document.

The Role of the Patient

A collaborative relationship requires that you are clear with the patient about your expectations. These expectations should include the following:

- To be an active participant. It is important to emphasize that the collaborative nature of this treatment requires the patient's engagement. Many patients may not know what it means to be an active participant. Help the patient by providing concrete examples. For example, the patient should come with questions and speak up in meetings. If the patient has some difficulty participating for any reason, he should discuss this with you.

- To be open with you. Explain to the patient that although you come with a certain expertise, he needs to be open with you about the difficulties he is facing.

- To provide feedback about the session. Explain that you will sometimes ask for feedback about what the patient has understood to be sure that you are both on the same page. You will also ask about the patient's satisfaction with the therapy. Emphasize that it is important that the patient let you know if there is anything he is unsatisfied with.

- To bring the workbook and a pen to all sessions. Encourage the patient to make notes in his workbook.

- To do the homework. Emphasize that patients who do homework benefit far more than patients who do not. The sessions alone do not magically create change. However, also emphasize that if the patient does not do the homework for some reason it is still important to come to the session. If the patient has difficulty with the homework, either because he doesn't understand something or just because he was not able to complete it, he should bring this up with you.

- To be patient and kind with himself. Explain that therapy takes both time and work, and therefore requires continuing effort and patience. To support himself, it is important that he reward himself for his hard work. Identify with the patient specific things he can do or say to himself as rewards for even small steps of success.

Therapist Note

■ *This would be a good time to demonstrate some elements of the collaborative relationship. Ask what the patient has understood about your respective roles, and how that sounds to the patient. Is there anything he would like to add to that, or anything he does not like?* ■

Rationale for Stress and Mood Management for MS

Most people with MS believe that stress makes their disease worse. In 1877, Charcot, one of the first to identify MS as a distinct disease, noted that emotional difficulties seemed to be related to the disease. However, throughout the remainder of the 1800s and early 1900s, while many researchers reported cases in which the symptoms of MS were associated with physical or emotional trauma, the medical community generally dismissed the idea that stress is related to MS disease activity. However, there is now research that indicates that stress may exacerbate MS.

Benefits

It is important to instill a sense of accurate hopefulness. The therapist should be accurate in describing benefits, not make absolute promises about what will happen with the individual patient, but describe the benefits that have been demonstrated by research (refer to chapter 1 for more information). The MS stress and mood management program has been shown to:

- Reduce mood problems like depression

- Decrease stress

- Increase well-being, quality of life, and positive emotions

- Increase satisfaction from relationships

- Improve ability to manage difficult relationships

- Reduce fatigue

- Possibly improve immune functioning related to MS

Some patients may press for a specific prognosis for themselves. Often such inquiries are driven by anxiety. You may initiate a discussion of those anxieties by saying something like:

> *Research has shown that people like yourself show significant improvement in* [particular area of patient's concern] *when they use the stress and mood management program. Are there reasons why you think you would not?*

Where Do Distress and Mood Problems Come From?

Problems with mood are more common among people with MS (Patten, Beck, Williams, Barbui, & Metz, 2003; Sadovnick, et al., 1996). There are many potential causes for these problems. The three major ones are stress, genetics, and MS. Discuss each of these factors, and then, most importantly, how they interact.

- **Stress:** Stressful events in our lives often result in distress—unpleasant feelings like depression, anxiety, or anger. But some people can experience a lot of stress and not develop depression, anxiety or feel too overwhelmed. Other people are more vulnerable to stress.

- **Genetics:** Some people are simply more likely to become depressed, anxious, or angry. But people who are genetically predisposed to feelings of depression, anxiety or feeling overwhelmed don't feel like that all the time. Usually, for these people, there needs to be a trigger. That is, a stressor needs to trigger it.

- **MS:** There is some evidence that distress and mood problems may be related to MS itself. The underlying inflammation associated with MS can increase the likelihood that people with MS will experience some of these symptoms. Thus, people with MS may be more sensitive to the effects of stress.

Emphasize that symptoms of distress and mood problems are likely an interaction among these factors. Stress is usually part of the equation. Many studies have shown that the stress management techniques described in this book help people with MS feel better (Mohr, Boudewyn, Goodkin, et al., 2001; Mohr, Hart, & Marmar, 2006).

What Is Stress and Where Does It Come From?

Explain to the patient that stress is an emotional, physical, or mental tension that results from something that is "outside" of us. We call these things "stressors" or "stressful life events." Typically, for something to cause stress, it has to have two characteristics:

1. For something to be a stressor, *it has to threaten something that is important and valuable to you.* For example, stressful events in the workplace can be stressful to the degree you believe they threaten your job (if valued) or threaten a relationship that is important to you (e.g. a conflict that potentially may damage a relationship with a colleague you like, or have to work with).

2. *You have to believe that you may not be able to manage or control the stressor effectively.* Things that you know you can manage usually do not create distress, even when they take some work.

Thus, most distress comes from things we believe are threatening in some way, and which we believe we cannot or may not be able to manage. Often, because we have little control over the actions of others, other people and relationships are a large source of stress. Most commonly, these interpersonal problems involve family, work, and friends. Because money is what allows us to have the basic necessities of life, financial concerns are often another major source of stress. These kinds of concerns are pretty common for most people. People with MS experience all of these stressors. However, MS can also cause additional stressors.

Introduction to Stress and Mood Management for MS

Explain the stress and mood management model (see Figure 3.1). The following is an example of language that can be used:

There are many components to how we respond to stressful events. Usually we have some thoughts about the event. These thoughts may be threatening (e.g. "This is really going to mess me up") or challenging (e.g. "This may be tough, but I know I can get through this"). We often have emotional responses such as anxiety, anger, irritability, depression, or hopelessness. Commonly we also do something in response to stress, either something to fix the problem or something else to take our mind off the problem and help us feel better. Many times we have a physical reaction, sometimes noticeable and sometimes not (e.g. muscle tension, change in heart rate). Finally, stressful events often occur in the context of our social lives and prompt us to do something that involves other people (e.g. get angry, avoid people).

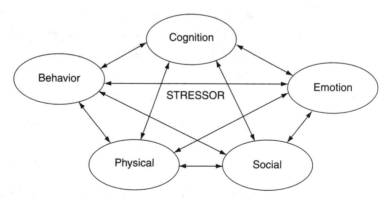

Figure 3.1
Stress and mood management model.

Five Areas of Responses to Stressful Life Events

Review the five categories of stress response; all of these can be easily seen when looking at the diagram of the stress and mood management model (Figure 3.1).

1. Thoughts (cognitive): Interpreting the event as a threat or a challenge, worrying, being more forgetful, having more difficulty concentrating, etc.

2. Emotions: Feeling tense, anxious, angry, irritable, restless, sad, hopeless, etc.

3. Behaviors: Avoidance of tasks, working more or less, increasing or decreasing eating, taking steps to fix the problem, taking steps to manage the emotional reaction, etc.

4. Physical Symptoms: Muscle tension, change in heart rate and blood pressure, increased fatigue, increased pain, changes in bowel function, headaches, stomach aches, etc.

5. Social Interactions: Avoidance of others, seeking people out, venting to other people, asking for help, trying to help others, etc.

Some astute patients may notice that social interactions can be the same as behaviors. If a patient asks about this, agree with him. However, social behavior and occurrences are included separately because social behavior is a very unique type of behavior that can have unique effects on health.

Example

Use the following example to illustrate the stress and mood management model:

Suppose you are at home, and the person you live with (spouse/partner/roommate) comes home, slamming the door as he/she walks in. You might think "He/she must be mad at me for something" (thought). That might cause you to feel anxious (emotion). Your cognitive and emotional reactions might cause your heart rate to speed up (physical symptom). At this point you might greet this person (behavior) in a defensive or angry way (social interaction). So you see how each of these can affect each other.

Now imagine that you learn that he/she has just had a big argument with his/her boss. What happens? You might suddenly think "Oh, this has nothing to do with me" (thought). Your anger or defensiveness would probably quickly drop and you might feel some compassion (emotion). Your heart rate would drop (physical symptom). You might even ask your (spouse/partner/roommate) if he/she is OK (behavior & social interaction).

There are several points to this story; review these with the patient.

- All of these stress reactions (thoughts, emotions, behaviors, physical symptoms, and social interactions) are interrelated.

- Stress reactions are not permanent. They change and eventually go away.

- If you change one of the stress reactions, you influence all the others. In the example, a realization (thought) about the reason for the person's behavior affected all the other responses.

- Depending on the problem, you can also change your behavioral, physical, and social reactions. Emotions are a little harder to control directly (with the exception of medications), but you can influence emotions indirectly through the other stress responses, particularly by what you do (behavior) and how you think (thoughts).

After presenting the example, ask the patient if he can think of any recent similar stressful situation. Examine with the patient how the stress reactions interacted.

Reversing the Vicious Cycle

An important idea in CBT is that these five components have an influence on one another. A negative thought stemming from an unpleasant event can cause negative feelings, and can change the way you react to people around you, which in turn can cause new negative thoughts and behaviors. In some instances these components can start a vicious cycle of negative changes, in which one thing feeds on another, leaving the patient feeling worse and worse. The goal of this program is to turn this vicious cycle around, and to create beneficial cycles—cycles in which the positive effects of the five components support and reinforce each other.

To illustrate this point, the workbook uses the preceding example of a partner coming home and slamming the door. In the session you might ask if the patient has an example of a situation in which a vicious cycle might have been turned around if the patient had done something different or interpreted or thought about an event in a different way.

Role of Homework

Tell the patient that each week he will be assigned "homework." You may want to use the terms "home tasks" or "home assignments" instead. Let the patient know that, unlike in school, you will work together to be sure home practice is the best it can be. Furthermore, the patient will be the ultimate judge of the success of his practice.

Reading chapters of the workbook will usually be one of the task assignments. Encourage patients to take notes and write down their thoughts in the workbook.

Importance of Homework

Inform the patient that considerable research has shown that doing homework greatly improves the success of stress management training (Kazantzis, Deane, & Ronan, 2000). While showing up for meetings is critically important, only showing up without doing the homework will not help much. Emphasize that there is no magic here—practice is necessary to make these new skills a routine part of the patient's daily life.

Problems with Homework Completion

Many circumstances make it difficult to complete homework. For example, time constraints, the difficulty of assignments, or fears of doing it "wrong" commonly interfere with completing assignments. Some people may not like someone else "telling them what to do," and sometimes people think that the assignment is silly, or useless. Remind patients that there is no wrong way to do homework. Some assignments may seem less helpful than others; however, they will not know if the assignment is helpful unless they try it. Some tasks are time-consuming, so patients may need to plan to set aside the time to do them.

Encourage patients to share their thoughts with you if they feel uncomfortable, uncertain, or skeptical about a task. Problem solve with the patient any obstacles to completing homework.

Session Summary

Approximately 5 min before the end of each session begin the summary. The summary should contain two parts: feedback and the actual summary.

The purpose of the feedback is to ensure that you and the patient agree on the process of the therapy. Ask the patient how the session was for him. Most patients are hesitant to criticize. Pull for it by asking "Is there anything we might do differently? Anything that was not what you expected or not what you wanted? Anything you would like us to do that we did not do?" and so on.

The summary is used to ensure that the patient understands the content of the session. Many therapists find it helpful to take notes to aid with the summary. Ask the patient what he understands to be the main take-home points of the session. Encourage the patient to ask questions. Correct any misconceptions and fill in any gaps. At the beginning of treatment you may be the one providing much of the summary. As time goes on, the patient should become better able to provide accurate summaries.

Homework

  Have the patient read chapter 1 of the workbook.

Chapter 4 *Problem Solving and Goal Setting*

(Corresponds to chapter 2 of the workbook)

Materials Needed

- Copy of patient workbook
- Goal and Action Plan Worksheet

Outline

- Set the agenda
- Rate the patient's stress/distress level
- Review homework
- Introduce problem solving and goal setting
- Summarize the session
- Remind the patient of the time and date of the next appointment
- Assign homework

Setting the Agenda

Begin by asking the patient if there is anything she would like to include in the agenda. In the early sessions it is usually necessary for you to take most of the responsibility for setting what you think will be a useful, productive agenda. But as the patient becomes acquainted with the program, it is good for the patient to take more and more responsibility for setting the agenda. This helps the patient learn the important components of stress and mood management, and underscores that the patient is ultimately responsible for implementing her own stress management program. If a patient does not add anything to the agenda, encourage her to add something; what does she want to talk about today? After writing down the list, *prioritize* the items (and later on, it's good to add projected amounts of time to each item so that the session moves along and every topic gets some coverage during the session).

Review of Stress or Distress

Have the patient rate her level of stress or distress on the 1–10 scale. Note with the patient if the level is higher, lower, or the same as the previous week. Ask the patient for thoughts as to why she thinks her stress/distress is higher, lower, or the same. Help the patient form thoughts about the stress and mood management model. Even though thought restructuring has not yet been addressed (see chapter 7 for more information), begin helping the patient look for the cognitive, behavioral, and social antecedents.

Homework Review

Review any homework you may have given, including reading the corresponding workbook chapter. If the patient completed the reading, ask if she has any thoughts or questions.

If the assigned task wasn't done, discuss the problem encouraging the patient to describe the obstacles that interfered with the task. These may include lack of clarity of assignment, lack of time on the patient's part, lack of motivation, no real belief in the model. Elicit reasons and respond within a stress and mood management framework.

It is important that the patient knows that homework review will be a *recurring part of every session*. Even if this was not a big assignment, it is important to give the patient the message that completing homework is integral to treatment.

Problem solving has two functions in stress and mood management therapy. First, setting goals helps keep the therapy on target, and helps both you and the patient maintain a consistent direction. Patients who are distressed frequently come into sessions wanting to deal with their most recent problem. While it is important to help them manage these stressors, it is also important to help them make progress on larger goals. If a person can make progress in resolving a problem, this will have ripple effects in terms of improving mood, strengthening a sense of self-efficacy in tackling other problems, and improving the patient's skills in managing stressors more generally.

The second purpose of introducing problem solving at this stage is to begin changing the patient's behaviors. Frequently, distress and depression are maintained in part by behaviors that do not resolve, or often contribute to, the distress (the vicious cycle introduced in chapter 3). Helping patients begin to initiate more helpful behaviors is a first step toward reversing the vicious cycle.

The first step in developing helpful goals and action plans is to identify target complaints or as they are referred to in the workbook, "problems." These target complaints or problems should be delineations of situations that are troublesome, so that specific, actionable behavioral goals for change can be set. Often patients frame their problems in ways that are vague and do not help identify helpful goals. For example, defining a problem as "I am depressed" does not move the patient any closer to finding goals and developing useful action plans. To assist the patient in identifying problems and framing them in a helpful way, you may wish to ask the following questions:

- Who is involved in the problem?

- What makes this a problem?

- When does the problem occur and under what circumstances?

- Where does the problem occur?

- How often does the problem occur?

- What causes the problem or makes it worse?

Ask the patient to use the space provided in the workbook to list three main problems she is confronting. Help the patient select one problem to focus on. Ask the patient to rank problems in order of most distressing to least distressing and to choose a problem that ranks in the middle. The purpose of this exercise is to select a problem that is meaningful to the patient, but one that is likely to result in a success experience.

Translating Problems into Goals—Using the Goal and Action Plan Worksheet

The Goal and Action Plan Worksheet outlines three basic steps: (1) identifying a helpful goal, (2) developing an action plan, and (3) monitoring results of the action plan.

Characteristics of Helpful Goals

In the workbook we use the term "helpful," rather than "good" when discussing goals and action plans to deemphasize value judgments (i.e. good vs. bad) and to emphasize their purpose. Patients often have difficulty identifying helpful goals. Indeed, if it were easy to identify helpful goals, they would have likely done so already. There are two characteristics of helpful goals. Review these with the patient.

Attainable

A helpful goal is something that is attainable. A useful goal is usually framed in such a way that it can be accomplished within a few weeks and not more than 2–3 months. When choosing the first goal, however, it is better to work toward a goal that can bring positive effects within a week or two.

Positive

A helpful goal is one that moves the patient toward something positive, not just away from the problem. A useful question to assist the patient in identifying a helpful goal is:

- If the problem didn't exist, how would your life be different?

When the patient has identified a helpful goal, ask her to write it down on the Goal and Action Plan Worksheet provided in the workbook.

Developing an Action Plan

Action items are specific behaviors that will move the patient toward her identified goal. The sections follow describe some of the characteristics of helpful action items.

Feasible

A helpful action item is something that is feasible—something that a person can expect to accomplish within a reasonable amount of time. Usually an action item should be framed in such a way that it can be accomplished within a day. If it takes longer than that, it should be broken down into smaller achievable steps. If a person wants to clean a house that has become very disorganized and chaotic, helpful action items that can be accomplished in a few hours would be "pick up the living room," "pick up the bedroom," "organize the desk," and so on.

Under Your Control

Action items should be behaviors that patients can do on their own and not things that are dependent upon other people's behaviors.

Time-Specific

The patient should schedule a specific time to complete each action item. If that is not realistic, the patient should schedule a deadline by which the action items will be completed. Scheduling will increase the likelihood that the patient will complete all items.

Strategies for Coming up with Helpful Goals and Action Items

Coming up with helpful goals and action items is often difficult for patients. Your job as the therapist is to help the patient become good at developing helpful goals and actions items and to use available resources. Only after you do that should you provide any suggestions. A number of strategies for developing helpful goals and action items are provided in the patient workbook.

Monitoring Progress

The process of change involves setting a goal, implementing a plan, monitoring the success of the plan, and modifying the goal or plan as needed. Accordingly, it is important that the patient keep track of whether she is making progress on her action plan. Section 3 of the Goal and Action Plan Worksheet includes several questions that the patient should ask herself each week. These are:

- How satisfied are you with your progress? If your progress is not 100%, was it acceptable?

- Were there any obstacles to completing your action items?

- If so, what can you learn from those obstacles, and how can you avoid them in the future?

- Do you need to make any changes to your action plan?

Changing the Action Plan

As the patient works toward her goals, it may become apparent that the initial action plan is not successful or could be improved. Sometimes the changes are small, such as allowing more time to complete items. Other times, more patience and time is required for the action plan to work. And, in some cases the patient may have to go back to the beginning and create an entirely new action plan. Remind the patient that as the action plan is developed and modified, she is learning how to more effectively reach her goals.

Follow-up and Setting New Goals

It is important to follow up on the goals. We recommend that each week the homework assignment include some step toward goals. We also recommend reviewing Goal and Action Plan Worksheets at each session.

Summary of Session

The importance of summaries was discussed in chapter 3. Obtain feedback from the patient on how the session went.

Ask the patient to summarize the session. Some useful questions are

- What has the patient learned?

- What new skill has she learned?

- What homework assignments help the patient practice the skills learned in this chapter?

- Are there any additional thoughts or questions about the material?

Fill in any gaps or inaccuracies in the patient's understanding.

Reminder of Time and Date of the Next Appointment

It's good early on to set up the full session schedule with the patient if at all possible, so that times and days of the week become "regular" for you both. Laying out all the following planned sessions can also be helpful in reassuring your patient that therapy will go on, even if the patient is not responding yet or doesn't know how helpful it will be.

Homework

✎ Come to an agreement with the patient on how many goals she will develop. Ask the patient to complete that number of Goal and Action Plan Worksheets.

✎ Have the patient read chapter 3 of the workbook.

Chapter 5 | *Positive Activities*

(Corresponds to chapter 3 of the workbook)

Materials Needed

- Copy of patient workbook
- Activity Diary
- Positive Activities List form
- My Activity Scheduler form
- List of Pleasant Activities form

Outline

- Set the agenda (as per instructions in chapters 3 and 4)
- Rate the patient's stress/distress level (as per instructions in chapters 3 and 4)
- Review homework (including patient goals and action plans)
- Discuss the importance of positive activities
- Discuss the relationship between activities and mood
- Have the patient make a list of positive activities
- Have the patient schedule positive activities
- Encourage the patient to notice positive events
- Summarize the session
- Assign homework

Ask the patient to set the agenda. Add necessary items. Note that if the patient is depressed, it is best to break this chapter into at least two sections: Do activity monitoring with the Activity Diary the first week and activity scheduling the second week. Noticing positive events can be done either week—you can discuss scheduling this with the patient.

Ask the patient to rate his stress or distress on the 1–10 scale and compare it to the level of previous weeks.

Homework Review

In many ways, the homework review is the *most important* part of the session. While the rest of the session is mainly instructional, the homework is where "the rubber meets the road." It is where the patient begins implementing the new skills in his environment and life. Homework is where the patient struggles with the concepts, with barriers to making the changes, and with ambivalence. It is where the patient has the possibility of making the changes that can profoundly impact his quality of life. The homework review is your opportunity to review with the patient how he is doing with this critical part of the program. In general, you should:

- Find out if the patient completed the homework. If he did not, use this as an opportunity to explore what barriers the patient may have to completing homework, whether they are practical, like not having enough time, or psychological. Come up with a plan for overcoming the barriers.

- Review homework with the patient.

- Assess for obstacles or difficulties in completing the homework.

- Allow the patient to describe his successes and praise the patient for his work.

Review Goal and Action Plan Worksheets and any other homework that may have been assigned. Many people have difficulty coming up with helpful goals. If the patient's goals do not truly meet the characteristics of helpful goals, review these characteristics with the patient and help him come up with better goals.

Importance of Positive Activities

Positive activities are particularly useful for patients with depressive symptoms. A growing literature indicates that behavioral activation is extremely helpful for depression (Dimidjian et al., 2006). Patients who are overwhelmed, or stressed because they have too much to do, may not believe they have time for pleasurable activities in their lives. In addition, you should be aware that fatigue is extremely common in this population, further constraining the capacity for activity (refer to module 2 on fatigue for more detail). In these cases, part of the discussion with the patient may center on making choices about which activities are important to maintaining quality of life, and which activities are perhaps not enjoyable but necessary.

Ask the patient if he feels he could benefit from more pleasant events and activities in his life. Explain that this program will help patients decrease distress and increase positive emotions by increasing positive events. This entails four steps:

1. Learn the relationship between activities and mood by monitoring your activities and mood.

2. Identify things that are pleasurable and rewarding.

3. Increase your positive events by scheduling pleasurable and rewarding activities.

4. Learn to pay more attention to the positive events and experiences around you.

The Relationship between Activities and Mood

Review the relationship between activities and mood. Ask the patient for examples from his life that illustrate how stressful or unpleasant events can affect mood, as well as how positive events can affect mood. Explain that the first step is for the patient to carefully monitor his mood and activities so that he can learn how the things he does affect how he feels. If it is difficult to generate useful examples from the patient's life, you may want to use the case example of Janice in the workbook to demonstrate. Refer to Janice's completed Activity Diary (Figure 3.1 in the workbook), which includes ratings for Janice's mood at several key points during the day and identifies the situations that occurred at the time she rated her mood.

Keeping an Activity Diary

Have the patient practice completing a blank Activity Diary in session (a copy for the patient's use is provided in the workbook). This will help ensure that the patient understands how to complete this, using the following instructions:

1. In the first column, write the time of day for the activity you want to describe.

2. In the second column, write down the things that you did over the course of the day. Try to list at least five activities—the more the better. Don't worry if they are not big things. Even sitting and watching TV is a good thing to list.

3. Label the main feeling or feelings you had during and directly after those activities.

4. Rate how good/positive or bad/negative you felt on a scale of 0 to 10. If you felt "so-so," mark a 5. And if you felt low or depressed, mark a lower number.

5. In the space next to your mood rating for each day, please briefly give two major reasons why you think you felt that way. Try to be as specific as possible.

6. After you are done, review this chart using the questions in the next section.

For homework this week, the patient will complete an Activity Diary each day for 3–7 days. Ask the patient to pay attention to the events that surround his moods and record those events that contributed to his mood score. Also encourage the patient to pay attention to those holes in his life pattern when he might be able to do things that are a little bit more positive.

Review of Activity Diaries

Instruct the patient to review his Activity Diaries every few days to look for patterns. Review the example of Janice in the workbook. Also, review the patient's completed diaries in session. Ask the following questions:

- "Do you feel worse at certain times of day? In the morning or in the evening?"

- "Are certain activities or types of activities associated with better moods?"

- "Are negative moods connected to activities and events that are unpleasant and unrewarding?"

- "Is a poor mood connected to the absence of positive events?"

- "Are there holes in your schedule—'downtime'—when you do not have much to do, and when you feel down or distressed?"

Note that it will be useful to use these questions when reviewing the homework at the next session with your patient.

Therapist Note

- *Often when people feel down or stressed, they watch television or surf the Internet to "unwind." For most people, watching television is a fairly passive activity, while surfing the Internet can make time pass unnoticed. These activities are easy to do, but many people find that after doing these activities for long periods of time, they end up feeling worse. If a patient watches television or surfs the Internet on a regular basis, have him keep close track of how it affects his mood. If he finds that it does not help his mood, encourage him to begin finding other things he can do to replace television that are better for his mood.* ∎

Making a List of Positive Activities

Therapist Note

∎ *Patients should complete 3–7 days of Activity Diaries before continuing to activity scheduling. Particularly for patients who are depressed, it may be better to introduce activity scheduling in a second session, preferably scheduled 3–4 days later.* ∎

Describe the importance of positive activities in managing mood. Following is a rationale from the workbook that you can use for positive activities with the patient:

> *In the rush of daily life, many people start putting enjoyable activities way down on the priority list. There may be many activities you have abandoned because of competing demands, feeling overwhelmed, or for other reasons. On the other hand, you may want to participate in more pleasant activities but are unsure about how to start.*

Ask the patient to think about the types of activities that he finds pleasant, satisfying, or enjoyable. It may be difficult for patients that are depressed or have significant anxiety to think of activities that are pleasurable, as loss of motivation is one of the symptoms of these mood problems. Also, patients with growing numbers of symptoms or disabilities that interfere with activities may have more difficulty thinking of positive activities. This is particularly true if the patient has lost the capacity to engage in activities that were highly meaningful or important to him. If this is the case, review with the patient what those positive activities were. With the patient, try to understand what it was about the activity that was pleasurable. See if there are other ways to meet those needs. See the section on changes in self-image in chapter 2 for further discussion.

Positive activities should be activities that can be done in the course of day-to-day life (e.g. going to the movies or going to the beach for a day, as opposed to going on a 2-week safari). Have the patient list 5–10 things he enjoys doing that can be done in day-to-day life on the Positive Activities List form in the workbook. Have the patient rate how pleasant or satisfying each activity is on a scale of 1–10, and indicate how often he has done the activity in the recent past (e.g. three times per week, once in past month). See Figure 3.2 in the workbook for an example of a completed list for the case study of Janice.

See if the patient can generate a few positive activities in the session. If the patient has difficulty thinking of any activities, give the following suggestions:

- Remember back to when you were less down or stressed. What were the things you enjoyed or found rewarding then?

- Do a search on the Internet. If you search under "fun things to do," you will find many lists. If you add the area where you live, you may find more specific things to do in your area.

- Call a friend and say you want to get together—see if that person has any ideas for something to do.

Increasing Positive Activities

The next step after identifying personal positive activities is for the patient to actually begin participating in such tasks. Encourage the patient to try slowly introducing such activities into his schedule, beginning with one or two activities. If the patient plans to do too many activities, there may be a higher risk of not doing them, which may lead to disappointment or frustration. Make sure the patient's goals are attainable.

Review with the patient each of the following three steps:

1. Scheduling positive activities

2. Doing positive activities

3. Monitoring positive activities

Step 1: Scheduling Your Positive Activities

Provide the rationale for scheduling positive activities. Following is an example from the workbook that you can use:

Scheduling positive activities is an important step toward increasing enjoyment and a sense of accomplishment in your life, improving your mood, and decreasing your distress. Scheduling helps remind you to do the activities. Scheduling also indicates that these activities are important. You are making an obligation to yourself and for yourself; start increasing your positive activities and getting more control over your mood and distress. Obligations to yourself are no less important than obligations to anyone else!

Finally, scheduling helps organize your time so other things do not interfere with your positive activities.

If the patient uses a daily planner, have him use it to schedule at least one positive activity per day. The workbook also provides a planner form (My Activity Scheduler). Encourage the patient to put his planner or reminders someplace that is easily seen, like on the refrigerator. The patient should choose things that are not difficult to do. These activities do not need to be big things, or things that take a lot of time, especially at the start. It is more important for the patient to start scheduling things he can and will do than scheduling big things that he may not be able to do.

Help the patient plan or choose activities that he is likely to engage in without many obstacles. For example, if a patient likes going for walks but experiences increasing fatigue throughout the day, plan the walk earlier in the day.

Step 2: Do Your Positive Activity

The second step is to actually do the positive activity. There are two common issues that may interfere with completing positive activities.

■ It is common for people who are stressed or distressed to not feel motivated to do anything, even if it is potentially enjoyable. It is important to begin doing these activities, even if the person does not *want* to engage in them. A helpful way to frame this is that people usually expect to be motivated before they engage in an activity. But when a person is trying to make these kinds of changes, often he must take action before he feels motivated to do so. Hence the phrase *"action before motivation"* is used in the workbook. For patients who have difficulty with motivation, make this phrase a mantra.

- The second issue to anticipate is that the patient may not find the "positive event" all that enjoyable at first. Again, particularly for patients with depressive symptoms, anhedonia—the absence of the capacity to enjoy—is a common symptom. Anticipate this for the patient. That way, if he in fact does not enjoy the positive activity, he will understand why and be less likely to be demotivated by the experience.

Be aware that for some patients with a type of cognitive impairment called "executive dysfunction," one symptom may be more difficulty initiating behavior. That is, their MS has affected parts of their brain so that it is harder for them to start doing things. However, some research suggests these patients may do particularly well in this type of treatment (Julian & Mohr, 2006). For these patients, getting more active is a key to starting to feel better.

Step 3: Continue to Monitor Your Activities

After the patient has begun scheduling positive events, have him continue to monitor his activities and mood using the Activity Diary. The patient should include the activities he scheduled for himself. Encourage the patient to be on the lookout for ways to use activities to feel better. Mention the following:

Keep track of activities that leave you feeling better—even if it is only a bit better. If you find things you can do help your mood, see if you can do them more often. Add them to your positive activities list.

Start scheduling positive activities when you tend to feel down. Notice times during your day when you are feeling worse. As the workbook suggests, if you feel worse in the morning, you might try leaving the house a bit early and having your morning coffee out in a café. If you feel worse when things quiet down in the evening, see if you might meet or call a friend in the evening, or perhaps there is an activity you could get involved in one or two evenings per week? If you find you have downtime in which you are not doing much, but feel down or distressed, try scheduling or engaging in positive activities.

Noticing Positive Events

Explain to the patient that people who are generally happy have about the same number of stressful life events as do people who are unhappy. Although the occurrence of stressful or otherwise negative events creates distress, it is not all that big a factor in how happy or satisfied people are overall. One big difference between people who experience a lot of positive emotions and those who do not is that people who experience more positive emotions pay attention to positive or enjoyable events. You may want to use the following explanation from the workbook:

Noticing positive events does not necessarily mean the big things, although that is important too. Sometimes these can be the smallest of things—a smile from a stranger, a nice interaction with a colleague or friend, or just seeing something beautiful. Most of the time we do not even notice these pleasant events. Or if we do notice, we quickly forget. Focusing attention on these positive events will increase positive emotions like contentment or happiness.

Sometimes we discount positive events. This can happen with events both big and small. How common is it that people have some form of achievement, such as a raise or on an honor, and then reduce the positive emotions by telling themselves that they did not deserve it, or by finding something negative in it, such as focusing on the increased responsibility? Or in smaller ways—like if a person smiles at you, you wonder if they're just oddly friendly. See if you can start to catch how you might sometimes undercut your ability to gain pleasure from the positive events that occur around you.

Emphasize that an important part of noticing positive events is being aware of what one *experiences* as a result of an event. Have the patient complete the List of Pleasant Activities form in the workbook to help raise awareness of what he does on a daily basis that may be pleasant or enjoyable. It is very common for people to feel as though they were on "automatic pilot," just going through their daily routine without being aware of doing many of the activities.

The patient should also rate the amount of pleasure he experienced to begin to underscore the link between noticing positive events and positive mood.

Summary of Session

Ask the patient for feedback on the process of the session, including what went well and what might have gone better. Also, ask the patient to summarize the content of the session. As the therapist you can fill in what the patient may have missed or misunderstood.

Homework

Ideally the patient will complete an Activity Diary each day. Have the patient identify a time of day when he is able to do this. Identifying a specific time increases the likelihood of completion.

If the patient is depressed, consider putting off the following homework assignments until the following session.

After at least 3 days, have the patient begin reviewing his Activity Diaries.

Have the patient start making his Positive Activities List.

After having analyzed 3 days of Activity Diaries, have the patient begin scheduling at least one positive activity per day and continue recording in his Activity Diary.

Encourage the patient to notice the positive events that occur spontaneously in his life.

Have the patient read chapter 4 of the workbook.

Discuss any assignments relevant to the patient's goals.

Chapter 6   *Identifying and Evaluating Unhelpful Thoughts*

(Corresponds to chapter 4 of the workbook)

Materials Needed

- Copy of patient workbook
- Unhelpful Thought Diary I and II

Outline

- Set agenda
- Rate the patient's stress/distress level
- Review homework (including goals and action plans)
- Review the stress and mood management model
- Introduce monitoring cognitions and emotions
- Discuss automatic thoughts and how to identify those that are unhelpful
- Teach patient to use an Unhelpful Thought Diary
- Discuss negative thought patterns, including identifying types of thought distortions
- Summarize session
- Assign homework

Therapist Note

■ *This chapter contains concepts that are difficult for some patients to grasp. It may take a few weeks of work. If that is the case, it is better to take the time to help the patient get it right, than to try to stick to some sort of schedule. For many patients, you may want to introduce the basic Unhelpful Thought Diary (UTD I) in one week, and the UTD II, which has space to record negative thought patterns, in another.* ■

Set the Agenda and Rate Stress/Distress

Ask the patient to set the agenda. Add necessary items. Ask the patient to rate her stress or distress on the 1–10 scale and compare to previous weeks.

Homework Review

Review the patient's completed Activity Diaries. Ask the patient if she noticed any patterns that predicted better or worse mood. Check for times of day, effects of activities involving interpersonal contact, effects of periods of time of no activity, etc. If the patient did not record activities, review what interfered with completing the assignment. Are there structural barriers or are the barriers psychological (e.g. concerns about what the therapist might think about the patient's chosen activities, or not wanting to see the activities displayed on paper)? Discuss ways to overcome barriers (e.g. scheduling a specific time to complete the Activity Diary, like right *before* settling in to watch TV in the evening). Complete an Activity Diary with the patient in session.

Review the patient's list of positive activities. If there are less than 5–10 items that are fairly doable, work with the patient to expand the list in session.

Review scheduled activities, if they occurred. Review how these activities affected the patient's mood. What would have the patient's mood been at those times if she had not engaged in these activities? If the patient did not schedule or engage in positive activities, evaluate what might be interfering. Have the patient schedule three activities over the coming days.

Review noticing positive events. What has the patient noticed over the previous week? Why does she think she does not notice these things, and what effect might this have on her mood, distress, and well-being? How can the patient change her attention toward positive events?

Review any other assignments that were agreed upon, including those aimed at goals.

Review of the Stress and Mood Management Model

Refer back to Figure 3.1 in chapter 3 (the stress and mood management model).

Briefly review with the patient the connection between thoughts, emotions, physical symptoms, behaviors, and social interactions and how each of these components interacts with the others, in both positive and negative directions. You may want to open this discussion by saying something like the following:

> When we want to make changes in our lives, any change we make in any of these components will likely change the other areas. For example, if you have started scheduling more positive activities and noticing positive events, this should lead to a better mood (emotions), a more positive outlook (thoughts), and maybe even changes how you feel physically and socially. Now we are going to start focusing on your thoughts. We all know that stressful events can make us feel bad, both emotionally and physically. But for most stressors, we cannot just reach inside of ourselves and change these feelings and sensations. We feel bad emotionally and physically because of what we think and how we interpret these events. For example, if you learn that two friends went to lunch and did not call or invite you, if you thought "They didn't want me around—they must find me boring," what would you feel? Now imagine you learned that the two of them had had an argument about something that didn't involve you, and they were meeting to talk about it—how would that change how you felt? (You may wish to use an example more relevant to the patient here if one is available.) Notice that it is the same event. It is your interpretation—your thoughts—that determine what you feel. If you can learn to identify those thoughts and learn to challenge those thoughts that are unfounded, distorted, or unhelpful, you will gain a powerful tool in

managing your stress, mood, and distress. Later on in treatment we will focus on how to assess, identify, and change your thinking.

Introduce to the patient the three basic steps to changing how we think:

1. Pay attention to and identify what you are thinking

2. Evaluate your thoughts

3. Change your thinking

This session focuses on *identifying* and *evaluating* thoughts. The next session looks at how those thoughts may fit into various common patterns, known as unhelpful thought patterns, and ways of changing unhelpful thoughts.

Automatic Thoughts

Introduce the concept of automatic thoughts to the patient. Be sure to underscore some of the points raised in the patient workbook. You may wish to say something like the following:

> *One of the primary things your brain does is produce thoughts. Just like your heart pumps blood, your brain continues to pump out thoughts. These thoughts go on in our heads all the time, sometimes with, and often without us really even paying attention. It is a lot like a TV that is on while we are in the next room. Sometimes we notice a phrase or a sentence. And sometimes the TV just continues without us even noticing. These thoughts that just keep coming are called "automatic thoughts." They have an effect on our mood and how we think about ourselves and the world around us, whether or not we pay attention to them.*

Helpful and Unhelpful Automatic Thoughts

Explain that people can have both helpful and unhelpful automatic thoughts. *Helpful thoughts* are those that lead to improved mood, enjoyable behaviors, and the successful accomplishment of individual goals.

Unhelpful thoughts create negative emotions, and can lead to problems with anxiety, anger, or depression. Explain that these thoughts sometimes are in response to big problems. Use an example from the patient's life if possible (e.g. "You mentioned that you had an argument with your sister. What did you think when that happened?"). Often it is just small things that trigger unhelpful thoughts. Again, elicit an example from the patient (e.g. "You mentioned that you hit a lot of traffic coming to the appointment today. What was going through your mind when that happened?"). And not uncommonly, unhelpful thoughts just come up on their own. Ask the patient for examples. If the patient needs prompting, ask about common times that these automatic unhelpful thoughts occur, such as in the middle of the night, or at times when the patient is minimally focused on something, like while driving. Underscore with the patient how frequently these unhelpful thoughts occur.

Importance of Awareness

Explain that our automatic thoughts often come so quickly that we are often unaware that we even had them before they start making us feel uncomfortable emotions. We are so used to having these unhelpful automatic thoughts that unless we make a conscious effort to notice them, we usually remain unaware of them and they continue to cause us problems. So the first step is increasing our awareness of these unhelpful automatic thoughts. Tell patients that the way to do this is to slow down their thoughts by keeping track of what they are thinking once they have noticed a strong emotional reaction. Gaining awareness of their thoughts will allow patients to choose how to respond to a given situation or stressor.

Using an Unhelpful Thought Diary

Introduce a core tool in monitoring automatic thoughts: the Unhelpful Thought Diary (UTD). The UTD is a tool designed to slow down the jump from stress to unpleasant feeling, and to help patients become more aware of their automatic unhelpful thoughts. The first type of UTD patients will use (UTD I) has four columns for the following information:

1. A brief description of the specific stressful event experienced

2. A list of the unhelpful automatic thoughts the patient had related to this event

3. A list of the unpleasant emotions that the patient experienced as a result of these automatic thoughts

4. A description of the physical responses that the patient experienced in response to this situation and the patient's subsequent automatic thoughts

Recording these four pieces of information on the UTD will help patients to practice noticing and monitoring the thoughts that immediately follow a stressful event. Illustrate with an example (see John's example UTD in chapter 4 of the workbook). Emphasize that the thoughts, feelings, and physical sensations can be entered in any order. The example of John in the workbook shows he was first aware of his anger and frustration and then identified his thoughts. But he then noticed a thought ("she doesn't care") that made him aware of feelings of disappointment.

The Strength of Unhelpful Thoughts

Another important component of the UTD is assigning some value or rating to thoughts to indicate the strength of the patient's belief in them. The rating exercise can help patients identify which thoughts are the most deeply ingrained and hardest to change. These ratings can also be used to compare the power of the patient's unhelpful thoughts as she progresses through the program (i.e. they should decrease in power as the patient learns to challenge them).

This rating utilizes a scale between 0 (not strong at all) and 10 (very strong). You may want to illustrate with the example of John's UTD in the workbook.

The Strength of Emotions and Physical Symptoms

Explain to the patient that just as it is important to measure the strength of her thoughts, it is equally important to measure the strength of her emotional responses to a given situation. The range of the rating scale is the same: 0 means that the emotion is not at all present and 10 means that the emotion is completely present, or as strong as it could possibly be. These ratings can help the patient identify which emotions are strongest, and help identify the thoughts that are most troublesome. These ratings will also be compared to subsequent ratings, which will be discussed in the next chapter (and which should hopefully improve as patients learn to change their thoughts). Similarly, it will be useful to track the intensity of any physical symptoms on the same 0–10 scale. You may want to point out that John's example UTD demonstrates that he rates his emotions of frustration and anger as very strong, with disappointment somewhere between moderately strong and very strong.

Practicing a UTD

It is very important to do one or two UTDs in session. Identifying accurate, useful unhelpful thoughts is very difficult for some patients, and can take some work on the part of the therapist. Elicit a fresh situation from the patient, preferably from the same day.

Therapist Note

■ *It is compelling to want to change these thoughts right away. It is okay for the patient to begin countering the unhelpful thoughts, but encourage him to focus on increasing awareness and identification of thoughts for now.* ■

Use the following checklist of steps (also provided in the workbook):

■ Identify the distressing event.

■ Identify your thoughts.

■ Rate (using a 0–10 scale) how strongly you believe in these thoughts.

■ Identify your emotions.

- Rate (using a 0–10 scale) how strongly you are experiencing these emotions.

- List any physical symptoms you might notice (muscle tension, jitteriness, fatigue, sweat, heart rate, etc.).

- Rate (using a 0–10 scale) the strength of any physical symptoms.

It may be hard for patients to identify thoughts at first. Some patients may have a hard time generating any thoughts. Others may generate thoughts that are confounded with feelings (e.g. "he made me mad"), are very superficial, or are more of a narrative about the stressful event. To help the patient identify unhelpful thoughts, ask her to identify:

- Automatic thoughts about the situation

- Automatic thoughts about oneself

- Automatic thoughts about other people

- Automatic thoughts about the future

Review some questions patients might ask themselves to identify automatic thoughts:

- What was going through your mind right after that event?

- What does this say or mean about you and your life?

- What does this say about your future? What are you afraid might happen?

- What does this say about people generally?

- What does this mean about your relationships with other people? About how they feel or think about you?

- What does this say about you?

Of course you should be creative in helping the patient discover her own thoughts and thinking processes. Discuss with the patient how easy or difficult it was for her to come up with the automatic thoughts associated with the stressful event and her negative emotions. If the patient found it difficult, offer reassurance that most people find that it takes practice to identify their automatic thoughts. Remind the patient that slowing down the thought process will make it easier to identify her automatic thoughts.

Patients sometimes begin spontaneously challenging their thoughts. You can praise them for anticipating the next step in the therapy process. However, it is important to spend the time to ensure the patient learns how to put together a good thought record. Do not let the patient get you off task.

If the patient has any difficulty identifying thoughts, consider stopping here and introducing the material on evaluating unhelpful thoughts (see section on Types of Negative Thought Patterns) the following week.

Negative Thought Patterns

Thought patterns are the lenses through which we view the world—characteristic ways of interpreting events in our lives. They are templates that help us organize information. However, when these patterns are distorted in a way that consistently leads to a negative bias in your interpretations and thoughts, they can lead to negative emotions including sadness, anxiety, hopelessness, distress, and a loss of motivation. We call these *negative thought patterns*.

Describe negative thought patterns to the patient. Now that she has been keeping track of her automatic unhelpful thoughts, she may have noticed a few patterns.

We have compiled a list of negative thought patterns that are common among individuals who are stressed, fatigued, depressed, or overwhelmed. Review this list with the patient (the same list is provided in the workbook). Let her know that people often find that some of these thoughts fit them better than others. Sometimes more than one pattern may fit. Also, this list is not exhaustive and the patient may find that she often uses a negative thought pattern that isn't included. The real goal is to just identify the patterns that the patient does use.

Types of Negative Thought Patterns

The following are adapted from *Feeling Good: The New Mood Therapy* (Burns, 1999).

All-or-Nothing Thinking (Black-and-White Thinking)

You think in black-and-white terms; there are no gray areas. This type of thinking is unrealistic because things are seldom all or nothing, good or bad.

Example: A person who is having difficulty completing a work assignment and is feeling ineffectual might think, "Everybody else seems like they are real go-getters; I don't seem to be able to do anything." This is an exaggeration, because clearly the person *can* do things.

"Should" Statements

You build your expectations with "shoulds," "musts," and "oughts." When you don't follow through, you feel guilty. When others disappoint you, you feel angry and resentful.

Example: For example, a person invited to the wedding of a cousin who she is not very close to thinks "I should be there for Linda's wedding even though I'm in the middle of an MS exacerbation."

Overgeneralization

You assume that a one-time negative occurrence will happen again and again. You use words like "always" or "never" to make generalizations.

Example: A person is running late for an early morning appointment, rushes to the car, gets in, and begins driving. Suddenly she realizes that she has forgotten her cell phone and tells herself, "This is going to be a really bad day." This is generalizing from a few events to the whole day.

Disqualifying the Positive

You turn positives into negatives by insisting they "don't count." This allows you to maintain your negative outlook despite positive experiences.

Example: If someone receives a compliment on her clothes or work, she might think, "Oh, they're just being nice." This discounts the fact that the person probably really meant what he said.

Jumping to Conclusions

In the absence of solid evidence, you jump to a negative conclusion. There are three types of this: "mind reading," the "fortune teller error," and "overinterpretation."

Mind Reading. You assume that you know what someone else is thinking. You are so convinced that the person is having a negative reaction to you, you don't even take the time to confirm your guess.

Example: A woman is at a busy holiday party and a friend interacts very little with her, and the woman thinks "She is ignoring me. She must be angry with me." In fact there are many people there whom the friend has not seen in a long time, and she figured the two of them see each other frequently.

The Fortune Teller Error. You act as a fortune teller who only predicts the worst for you. You then treat your unrealistic prediction as if it were a proven fact.

Example: A common example is thinking "My MS will probably get so bad that I'll end up helpless, alone, and incapacitated for the rest of my life."

Overinterpretation. You come to conclusions or interpretations that may be quite exaggerated.

Example: In the example of John, when his wife asks him to pick something up from the store he thinks "She isn't pulling her weight." Often these thoughts have a "should" thought behind them (e.g. "She should be doing more.").

Magnification (Catastrophizing)

You magnify negative things, blowing their importance out of proportion. The outcome of an event appears catastrophic to you.

Example: A married couple has an argument and one of the two starts thinking "Our marriage is really in trouble. It is only a matter of time before my spouse leaves me and I will end up being alone for the rest of my life."

Emotional Reasoning

You take your emotions as proof of the way things really are. You assume something is true because you feel it is.

Example: A parent thinks, "I'm feeling overwhelmed with raising my children. I must be a bad parent!"

Labeling and Name-Calling

You label yourself or someone else, rather than just identifying the behavior. Often when people engage in name-calling toward themselves, they are much harder on themselves than others would be, or than they would be toward others.

Example: A person whose MS symptoms are impacting her stamina might think "I'm such a loser for not getting everything done."

Personalization

You take responsibility for things that you don't have control over. You feel guilty because you assume a negative event is your fault.

Example: An example is blaming one's self for symptoms. "There's something wrong with me. It's my fault I am so fatigued all the time."

Tell patients to refer to this list as they monitor their thoughts in the coming week. Patients often readily identify with a few of these, and that is fine. One very useful function of identifying negative thought patterns is that by labeling the thought, it places distance between the patient and the thought. Creating this distance will allow the patient to be able to better evaluate the thought. Occasionally a patient will spend an inordinate amount of time trying to figure out which is the "right" thought pattern. This is counterproductive. Emphasize that there is no "right" answer. The goal is *not* to create something new for the patient to worry about. The goal is to make a quick determination of the negative thought pattern (or patterns) that is *reasonably* accurate.

Identifying Unhelpful Thought Patterns

Patients can use a new five-column UTD (UTD II) to identify unhelpful thought patterns. Use the example of John in chapter 4 of the workbook (Figure 4.2) to have the patient practice identifying unhelpful thought patterns.

Use one of the patient's previously completed UTDs to begin helping her identify negative thought patterns.

Summary

Ask the patient for feedback on the process of the session. Also, ask the patient to summarize the content of the session. As the therapist you can fill in what the patient may have missed or misunderstood.

The dark lines on the stress and mood management model (Figure 6.1) show the portions of the model covered so far. You may want to use the following dialogue to summarize:

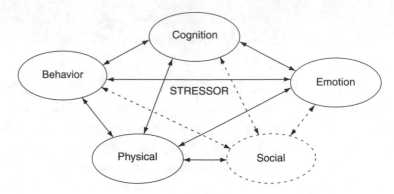

Figure 6.1

Stress and mood management model in progress

In the last chapter you began focusing on your behavior by increasing pleasant activities (behavior). Pleasant activities may put a more positive spin on your thoughts. In this chapter you learned about the connection between your automatic thoughts and your emotions. The homework this week will help you get better at noticing these links. You will also begin tracking how these thoughts affect you physically. In the next chapter you will begin to look at how to change unhelpful thought patterns. But first you need to practice becoming aware of these unhelpful thoughts as well as their distortions.

Homework

✎ Have the patient complete a four-column UTD (UTD I), recording thoughts and the accompanying emotions, physical reactions, and consequences.

✎ Have the patient begin using the new five-column UTD (UTD II) to identify negative thought patterns. Patient should continue to complete 1–3 UTD IIs for an additional 3–5 days.

✎ Encourage the patient to continue scheduling positive activities.

✎ Have the patient read chapter 5 of the workbook.

✎ Discuss any assignments relevant to the patient's goals.

Chapter 7 | *Challenging Unhelpful Thoughts*

(Corresponds to chapter 5 of the workbook)

Materials Needed

- Copy of patient workbook
- Challenging Your Unhelpful Thoughts Diary

Outline

- Set the agenda
- Rate the patient's stress/distress level
- Review homework (including goals and action plans)
- Address the issue of potential diminished enthusiasm for treatment.
- Teach ways to challenge and change unhelpful thoughts
- Introduce the Challenging Your Unhelpful Thoughts Diary
- Summarize the session
- Assign homework

Set the Agenda and Rate Stress/Distress

Ask the patient to set the agenda. Add necessary items. Ask the patient to rate his stress or distress on the 1–10 scale and compare to previous weeks.

Homewrk Review

Review the patient's completed Unhelpful Thought Diaries and address the following:

- Did the patient notice any recurrent automatic unhelpful thoughts?

- Did the patient notice any common negative thought patterns?

- Ask the patient what relationships he noticed between thoughts, emotions, and physical symptoms.

Review any additional homework, including any tasks related to goals.

Diminishing Enthusiasm for Treatment

People often begin stress and mood management programs with a lot of enthusiasm, but sometimes after 4 weeks or so, the novelty begins to fade, and sometimes discouragement may creep in. Evaluate if this is happening with the patient. If the patient continues to be enthusiastic, it is helpful to anticipate that at some point in the future he may become less motivated. This is normal. Anticipating future loss of enthusiasm can "inoculate" the patient against disappointment.

If the patient is feeling less motivated (or if this occurs in the future), it is important to take a few minutes to discuss this. People come to stress management programs because they want changes in their lives. But most people are hoping for a kind of magic bullet—a transformation of their lives that will eliminate their problems and create a sense of fulfillment. The beginning of treatment is often akin to a "honeymoon period." Usually, even when the honeymoon is over, people still expect positive changes, but the realization that it takes hard work to make these changes starts to sink in. Emphasize that making changes at this point is key to creating lasting change. Eventually old habits return—if one can make changes in the face of that, then real change is taking place! You may want to reiterate this point with material from the workbook:

> *It is as the honeymoon period ends that you are beginning to make the real changes in your life that will have a lasting effect. Making changes*

during the initial weeks—during the honeymoon—is usually easier. But it is as the glow wears off and you begin struggling with all the resistances, hesitancies, and doubts that you are actually finding ways of making more permanent changes.

It is often said that change requires two steps forward and one step back. If you slip, that is normal. Don't be disheartened. By talking about these difficulties openly in session, you will find new ways to overcome these problems.

Take some time to talk with the patient, to help him see that the reasons he initially started this stress and mood management program are still there. It may be useful to ask some of the following questions:

- "Why do you think you were enthusiastic at the beginning?"

- "If you have become less enthusiastic, why do you think that is?"

- "What do you want out of this program at this point, now that you have some experience with it?"

Challenging and Changing Negative Thoughts

Emphasize the importance of practice to the patient. As patients practice identifying their automatic thoughts, unhelpful thought patterns, and their accompanying emotions, physiological responses, and social consequences, the process of recognizing them should become easier.

After learning to identify the types of unhelpful thought patterns, the next step is for the patient to learn to challenge these thoughts and replace the unhelpful thoughts with more helpful ones. In this session, you will introduce several methods for patients to use as they begin to explore and investigate their negative thoughts. As patients become more and more adept at recognizing, challenging, and replacing their unhelpful thoughts, they will become better at assessing how realistic, or exaggerated, their unhelpful thoughts are.

The new methods of thinking and reasoning will teach patients to investigate the sources of difficult emotions and unhelpful thoughts and come up with solutions. Review the following set of techniques to start patients off on the task of challenging unhelpful thoughts.

Step 1: Awareness

The patient has been using the Unhelpful Thought Diary (UTD) to identify his patterns of automatic thoughts and their consequences. If the patient has been able to produce good UTDs, then he is becoming more aware of the existence and nature of his unhelpful thoughts. At that point you can move on to the next step of challenging unhelpful thoughts.

Step 2: Challenge and Change Negative Perceptions

Review the following list of techniques for challenging negative thought patterns. Inform the patient that not all of these are appropriate for all situations. The patient should try a few different techniques and see which is most helpful, or which provides the most insight. Some of these suggestions overlap with each other and, furthermore, this is not an exhaustive list. Encourage patients to be creative, as they might come up with other strategies that work better for them. You may wish to say something like the following to introduce the list:

> Next we are going to review a set of techniques to challenge your negative thought patterns. Some require you to perform actual behaviors in challenging your thoughts and others ask you to analyze the thoughts from a different perspective.

What's the Evidence?

Often, we think there is evidence to prove that the negative thoughts about ourselves are true. We don't even think that on the other side of the scales, there is a lot of contradictory evidence. This technique involves considering the evidence for both sides. If the patient has provided a completed UTD that would lend itself to examining the evidence, use that. If a useful example from the patient is not available, you can use the following example from the workbook:

> Let's say that you made a mistake at work or forgot to return a phone call to a friend and called yourself "stupid." If you were to ask yourself

what evidence you have that the thought that you are "stupid" is true,
you might list the mistake you made at work, or that you forgot to call
a friend. Then, if you asked yourself for the evidence that this
statement is NOT true, you might list your accomplishments at work,
and that most of the time, you do remember to call your friends.
Therefore, you can conclude that while you may make mistakes at
times (as everyone does), there are many things you do quite well. You
may then go back and ask yourself now how strongly you believe that
you are stupid.

Encourage the patient to gather additional information in order to challenge unhelpful assumptions about situations or people. If the patient isn't sure whether his automatic thoughts are just snap judgments made without much supporting evidence, he could try asking friends or family for their thoughts about certain situations.

Language

Explain that a lot of negativity comes from the language we use with ourselves. We often create labels for ourselves without considering the true definitions. Sometimes we believe that we must behave, think, or feel according to some "rules" whose origins are unknown. You may wish to say something like the following:

If you call yourself "stupid" after making a mistake, you are more likely
to feel worse about yourself. But if you really examined the definition
of stupid, you would see you couldn't possibly fit that definition.
Change the language to be more compassionate. For example, "I made
a mistake but I have learned and grown from it." You might even add
"I'll be less likely to make that mistake in the future."

What's the Rule?

Unhelpful thoughts sometimes come from underlying "rules" that tell the individual how he or others *should* behave. Identifying the rule helps the patient decide if it is a rule that can be modified. "Should" statements usually reflect an underlying rule. Often the patient is not immediately aware of the rule, but can grasp it fairly readily when a "should" statement is involved. If the patient has a "should" statement in his thought record, use that to identify and challenge the underlying rule. Otherwise, you might say something like the following:

> We all need rules to live by, but when the rules are inflexible and cause you distress, it is time to take a look at them. Often these rules involve "should" statements, like "I should be more outgoing." If you see such a rule in your unhelpful thoughts, it can be helpful to ask yourself "Is this a rule that is helping me?" "What would happen if I didn't have this rule, or if this rule were not so absolute?" Using this example, you might then find that a more helpful and accurate thought is "There's no rule that I should be outgoing. I'd prefer to be a little more outgoing under some circumstances, and maybe I can work on that." Often substituting "prefer" for "should" can help make a more flexible outlook on life.

Consider All Alternatives—Including the In-Betweens

Sometimes people who are stressed, overwhelmed, or depressed think only in extremes and forget to consider other options that may be open to them. The goal is to find a less extreme thought. Again, try to use an appropriate unhelpful thought generated by the patient. If none exists, you can use the following example from the workbook:

> Most of the time things are not absolutely black or absolutely white—they are some shade of gray in between. The situation or problem may not be good, but it may not be as bad as you imagine. For example, if someone is angry with you, it does not mean they hate you, that they will always be angry with you, that you are absolutely wrong, or that they are absolutely right.

Act "As If"

Suggest that when the patient is talking to himself in a harsh and negative way, it would be helpful to try acting "as if" he were someone he respects and admires. In response to one of the patient's unhelpful thoughts, have him consider the following:

How would that admired person talk if he were in your shoes? What might that person say? What might you say to yourself when acting "as if" you were that person? Or what would you advise that person if he had a thought like yours?

Usually "acting as if" feels false at first, like play-acting. Tell patients this is normal; however, as they continue to practice, they will find that they can adopt the role.

Credit the Positives

Focusing on the stress in one's life is one way to come up with negative interpretations. When we focus on the negative, we forget that positive events, thoughts, and feelings *do* occur. Using one of the unhelpful thoughts listed on the patient's UTD, ask him if there is anything positive he is ignoring with the unhelpful thought. Ask the patient to spend a few moments thinking of the more positive aspects of some recent events, or positive thoughts he has had lately. Next, have the patient think about the positive effects these events or thoughts have had on his emotions. Help the patient put the event or unhelpful thought into the larger context that includes both the positive and the negative.

Positive Statements

Along with crediting positive accomplishments and qualities, patients may also want to develop some positive, personal statements that they say to themselves when they are experiencing negative thoughts and negative emotions. For example, someone feeling very overwhelmed might say, "I am strong and capable of overcoming obstacles," or "I've dealt with this before, and I can deal with this again." People for whom religion or spirituality are important often find it helpful to draw on their beliefs and faith for positive statements.

Examine the Consequences of Your Thinking

Negative thinking can have very specific emotional, physical, OR social consequences. Help the patient explore these consequences using one of his unhelpful thoughts. Ask if there are any positive consequences of that kind of unhelpful thought. Often there is. For example, a patient who worries a lot may believe that worrying ensures he will not inadvertently miss something. Also explore the negative consequences, including the effect on mood, well-being, physical comfort and health, and social functioning. It may also be useful to ask the patient to list the advantages and disadvantages of an unhelpful thought on a sheet of paper.

Emotional Thinking

If a patient is excessively worried about a negative event happening, have him focus on discriminating between the realistic and emotional probability of the event occurring. The realistic probability is the actual probability. But often, for things that are more frightening, the level of worry increases. Sometimes being able to determine how much is realistic worry and how much is emotional can help reduce distress.

Additional Comments

Given the uncertainty associated with the course of MS, it is not surprising that MS patients often show considerable anxiety and worry. Worries about MS-related decline are common and distressing. Using some of these techniques for challenging and managing these thoughts can be helpful. But more specific work targeting the management of anxiety may be necessary. For patients with these concerns, or who generally show anxiety, module 3 on anxiety should be considered.

Challenging Your Unhelpful Thoughts Diary

You may have begun challenging some of the patient's unhelpful thoughts using the techniques just discussed. Once you have introduced the concepts, work through a Challenging Your Unhelpful Thoughts Diary with the patient. Show the patient the new six-column form.

Much of the information to be collected was also collected on previous forms, but this diary has been rearranged somewhat. Now the patient will record his negative thought patterns in the "Automatic Thoughts" column. There are new columns for Realistic and Helpful Thoughts and for Future Changes. An example of a Challenging Your Unhelpful Thoughts Diary is provided in the patient workbook (Figure 5.1). In session, it is best to use one of the patient's previous UTD entries as a jumping-off point for completing the new diary.

Help the patient complete the columns that are familiar (e.g. "Event", "Emotions", and "Physical Symptoms"). Then use the following instructions to complete the remaining columns:

- Identify more realistic thoughts. Questions that summarize and can prompt the implementation of the ways of challenging unhelpful thoughts are summarized toward the end of the workbook chapter. Encourage the patient to refer to these questions frequently. They include:

  - What's the evidence that the thought is true? What's the evidence that the thought is not true?
  - Look at the language. Is it overly harsh?
  - What are the rules? Are they unrealistic?
  - Is the thought extreme—is it black-and-white? What is an in-between thought?
  - Act as if. What would a friend or someone you admire tell you? Or if things were reversed, what would you tell that person?
  - Is there anything positive in your life or recent positive events that you are ignoring? Can you put this in a broader context?
  - What are the consequences of the unhelpful thought? What are the advantages and disadvantages?
  - What would your thoughts be if you were feeling better right now?

- List the more helpful or accurate thoughts in the Realistic and Helpful Thoughts column.

- Rerate the strength of belief in the unhelpful thoughts. This is done after the patient has identified more realistic thoughts.

- Rerate the strength of the emotions and physical symptoms experienced. Usually there is some improvement in emotions, physical symptoms, and a reduction in strength in the belief, albeit not always a lot. Let the patient know that even a little improvement is a good sign, and it takes a while to become good at this. Occasionally a patient will show no change. If this occurs, you can try rerating 5–10 min later. If there is still no change, engage the patient in a discussion by asking if he has any ideas why this process may not be working.

- Identify future changes. Ask the patient if there is anything he would do differently in the future as a result of the new thoughts. There may not always be changes to list in this column.

After the patient completes the Challenging your Unhelpful Thoughts Diary, ask for feedback on the exercise. If he found it difficult, reassure him that it is very common for people to have difficulty completing the diary for the first time. Even if the patient was able to come up with helpful responses to his negative thoughts, he may not have a great deal of confidence in these new thoughts. It is important to reassure the patient. You may wish to say something like the following:

> *Often it takes a while for more helpful thoughts to "sink in." You've had your unhelpful thoughts for quite some time. Think about your old, unhelpful thoughts as an old habit. Breaking any old habit requires a lot of hard work and patience. It is important to remember, though, that old habits can be broken. You CAN learn to alter your negative thought patterns and to adopt more realistic thoughts. You have already begun this process. Remember, though, it would be impossible for you to fully erase your old unhelpful thoughts after completing your first thought record. Are you willing to give it a shot?*

At this point, it is important that patients become aware that beliefs they thought would stay with them forever *can be changed*. Furthermore, the best way to make these changes is to practice. Encourage patients to get into the habit of completing a Challenging Your Unhelpful Thoughts Diary each time they are experiencing a stressful event. Let them know that they can use any piece of paper. Eventually the goal is to get to the point where the patient can engage this process in their heads. But for now, emphasize that it is important to put these thought diaries down on paper.

Summary

Ask the patient for feedback on the process of the session. Also, ask the patient to summarize the content of the session. As the therapist you can fill in what the patient may have missed or misunderstood.

Homework

✎ Have the patient complete at least one Challenging Your Unhelpful Thoughts Diary each day.

✎ Consider continuing to assign scheduling and monitoring of positive activities, particularly if depressive symptoms remain.

✎ Have the patient read chapter 6 of the workbook.

✎ Discuss any assignments relevant to the patient's goals.

Chapter 8 *Social Support*

(Corresponds to chapter 6 of the workbook)

Materials Needed

- Copy of patient workbook
- The People in My Life form
- The Support I Provide form
- Challenging Your Unhelpful Thoughts Diary

Outline

- Set the agenda
- Rate the patient's stress/distress level
- Review homework (including goals and action plans)
- Introduce social support, including benefits and different types
- Help the patient identify her support system
- Discuss things to consider in developing and using support
- Address problems with getting support needs met
- Summarize the session
- Assign homework

Set the Agenda and Rate Stress/Distress

Ask the patient to set the agenda. Add necessary items. Ask the patient to rate her stress or distress on the 1–10 scale and compare to previous weeks.

Homework Review

Review the patient's completed Challenging Your Unhelpful Thought Diaries in detail. Be sure the patient understands how to challenge the unhelpful thoughts. If there are any signs of difficulty, complete another thought diary in session.

Review any other homework assignments.

Social Support

Explain that social support refers to the emotional and practical comfort and help that we receive from other people. It is knowing that we are part of a community of people who love and care for us, and value and think well of us.

Benefits of Social Support

Human beings are social animals and as such, other people are as important to our survival as the food we eat. When we are not stressed, social support offers companionship, warmth, intimacy, entertainment, sharing, and much more. Social support under non-stressful conditions can help shape our self-identity and maintain our self-esteem. Under stressful conditions, social support can offer consolation, comfort, alleviation of loneliness, as well as help with chores, financial assistance, and other forms of practical aid.

Research shows that when people feel they have adequate or satisfactory support systems, they have better health (Uchino, 2004). For example, people who feel supported socially have been shown to have fewer colds, lower risk of heart disease, and are more likely to live longer. Among people with MS, people with low social support are more likely to show signs of MS inflammation in response to stress and distress, while people with high social support seem to be able to experience more distress without having MS inflammation (Mohr & Genain, 2004). Thus, social support offers people not only emotional comfort and practical help, but it may also offer resilience in the face of illness.

Types of Support

Describe the different types of support.

Support can mean many different things. There are many different kinds of support and ways that others can provide support to you. Some kinds of support are practical—such as providing information, medical advice, or financial help. Other types of support are less practical and more emotional—such as listening or providing a shoulder to cry on. People need both kinds of support. We will discuss several different types of support that tend to be relevant to people with MS.

Emotional Support

One of the most important types of support for people under stress or pressure is emotional support. Emotional support involves feeling connected with others, feeling understood, and sensing that others are available if needed. These are the people we call on when we are down, just to talk, or just to be with.

Emotional support is critical for everyone's well-being; people with chronic illnesses are no exception. However, an individual's need for emotional support is often ignored or misunderstood by families, the medical community, and even by the person who needs it. Because providing emotional support is usually a sign of a close relationship, seeking emotional support can be associated with fears of rejection, criticism, or being perceived as a burden. These thoughts and worries can lead people to withdraw from others or sometimes even feel irritated when others do offer help.

Information Support

Information support involves receiving information and gaining knowledge about the stressor we are facing. For example, with MS, being well-informed about diagnostic and treatment procedures, the latest research findings, advocacy groups, financial counseling, and, if one is so inclined, alternative therapies can provide not only a sense of hope and control but also practical solutions to everyday problems associated with MS. Conversely, a lack of information can allow us to imagine the worst, and may contribute to unnecessary fear, helplessness, and a sense of being overwhelmed. The National Multiple Sclerosis Society, health providers, the Internet, and other organizations are important resources for information support. A list of information resources is included at the end of the workbook.

Practical Support

Practical support refers to the support we receive from friends, family, coworkers, medical people, and any one else who assists us with *doing* things. This includes things like asking a friend or family member for help with everyday tasks such as completing a chore, getting a ride to the doctor, or doing some babysitting. It can also be asking a stranger to help with a flat tire or carry something. It can be difficult for some people to ask others for practical support. Unhelpful thoughts such as "I will burden the other person," "I am weak," or "Others will get tired of my asking for their help" may discourage people from seeking the support they need. Without support, we might spend too much time and energy on a task that exacerbates symptoms of pain/fatigue. This can become a vicious cycle by intensifying our sense of hopelessness and level of stress. Evaluating our unhelpful thoughts can help us identify whether our concerns are realistic or exaggerated. If our concerns are realistic, communication skills and problem solving can help us secure the practical support we need.

A specific case of practical support that may be important, depending on the patient's level of disability, is vocational/economic support. Sometimes people with MS require some changes in the work place or work schedule to be able to perform optimally. This type of support may involve rearranging one's work schedule for optimal performance, implementing environmental engineering (ergonomics), examining vocational rehabilitation opportunities, and assessing for disability eligibility. The goal of vocational/economic support is to help a person remain as self-sufficient as possible.

Belonging Support

Sometimes we just want someone to go to the movies with, or ask over for dinner. We may not want to talk about anything emotional or difficult. We do not need anything in particular—we just want companionship. This is sometimes referred to as *belonging support*, because it helps us feel like we belong in this world. Sometimes people who provide us this support are not people we feel very close to. They may not be people from whom we would ask much in the way of favors. But many of us just need people to hang out with from time to time. The importance of this type of support should not be underestimated.

Identifying a Social Support Network

After describing the different types of support, examine the patient's support structure by having her fill out the People in My Life form in the workbook. Have the patient write the names of people that can be relied on for each type of support. Note that some people may be in more than one category because they provide multiple types of support. Have the patient rate her level of satisfaction with the support offered by each person and make a note of the specific support offered, for example, "Can ask them to drive me to a doctor's appointment," or "Able to call and ask them to a movie," etc.

The purpose of this exercise is to

■   Help the patient identify areas, if any, where she might need to develop support

- See that some people are good at providing some types of support and not good at others

- Help the patient make the best use of people's strengths, and not ask people to provide types of support for which they are not well-suited

Use the material in the next section to review and analyze the patient's support network.

Things to Consider in Developing and Using Support

Who Provides What?

Discuss with the patient how different people are better at providing different types of support. To reach out for support successfully, it's important to focus on one's needs and determine who can best meet them. You may want to use the following illustration from the workbook:

> *If you ask your doctor to lend you money and a family member for a prescription, you would end up frustrated. That may seem obvious. But a lot of times we ask someone who is good at listening or maybe a good buddy to do something practical and they don't come through. Or sometimes we try confiding something emotionally difficult in someone who has been very helpful in other ways, and it just falls flat. Just like you wouldn't write off your doctor for not lending you money, it may not always be good to write somebody off just because they fail us in one area of support.*

Explain that getting the right support requires asking people to provide what they can do and *not* what they cannot. It is useful for patients to know which types of support people in their support systems are able and willing to provide, and which types they are not. Give the following examples:

> *One person may be good at listening to you, but not very reliable in helping you do things. Another person may be reliable in helping you with tasks, but is not as good at providing emotional support when you are upset.*

In addition, a person's ability to provide support can vary over time, depending on her own life circumstances.

Using the People in My Life form, ask the patient if there are examples of people who are very good at one type of support and not another. Has the patient ever asked people to supply a type of support at which they were not good? What happened? How did the patient react?

Do You Have Enough Support?

Explain that, ideally, we would want a number of people to provide each type of support. If we have multiple people that we can rely on for each type of support, it is more likely that we will receive the support we need at any given time. For example, relying on only one person in our network for practical support can increase the likelihood that the support person will "burn out."

Support When You Do Not Want It

Often people offer support when it is unwanted or unneeded. Use the following example to illustrate:

> *A common example is when a partner or friend offers healthcare advice when what you really need is either emotional support or help with the dishes. This is often difficult because the person offering the help is trying to be of assistance, but it is irritating to you.*

Ask the patient if she has experienced this. If so, what was the circumstance? What kinds of thoughts did the patient have about it? What did she do about it? Help the patient think about adaptive ways to manage these situations. The following example from the workbook can be useful:

> *In such instances, rather than asking the person to stop, it is usually helpful to acknowledge their good intentions, and then direct them toward something that you need. For example, "I know you are offering this advice because you want to help but I'm feeling too*

overwhelmed to talk about that right now. If you'd like to help, do you think you could help me with the dishes?"

Your Support Needs Are Probably Different at Different Times

Discuss with the patient how one's needs for support will vary over time. For example, during an exacerbation patients may find that their needs for both practical and emotional support increase. Recognizing that support needs fluctuate can be helpful in combating unhelpful negative thoughts such as "I will *always* need to depend on others."

Dealing with People Who Do Not Provide Support

Ask the patient if she has experienced people close to her who cannot or will not provide support. Although it is hard not to personalize it when we don't get the support we need, using the thought restructuring techniques learned in this program (chapters 6 and 7) will help the patient maintain a more realistic appraisal.

> *For example, when someone refuses or does not follow through in helping you, your automatic thoughts might lead you to feel rejected. However, using the techniques you have learned to both evaluate the type of distortion you might be making and challenge these thoughts can help you make a more positive interpretation. Perhaps this person declined to help you because she felt limited in her ability to provide support. It is also possible that they had conflicts. People's ability to provide support varies over time, depending on the stresses they are under. Failure to provide support at one point does not necessarily mean that the person can never provide support.*

It is important to acknowledge that the patient may have family or friends in her network who are consistently disinterested in providing support, and possibly even critical and rejecting. If this is the case, discuss the situation further. You can help the patient come up with ways to limit her interactions with people who are critical or rejecting in all areas of support.

Insufficient social support usually has two potential sources. Sometimes there is not enough support in the person's network. Often this is the case when people are isolated. The other reason is that people have difficulty accessing the support that is available. It is also possible that people have inadequate social support networks and they do not know how to access the support that is there. In this section we discuss this in terms of "reducing isolation" and "asking for support." Evaluate with the patient, using the People in My Life form, if the patient feels satisfied with the support she currently has available.

Therapist Note

■ *Do not take assertions that the patient has no support needs at face value. Many patients will deny having unmet support needs. While this may be accurate, it is also frequently a reflection of reluctance to acknowledge needs. Many people view needing social support as a form of weakness or as an indication of some form of personal failing.* ■

Explain that many things can interfere with one's ability to get and use support effectively:

- Your thoughts and attitudes about asking for help

- Your emotions

- Your own behavior (e.g. a tendency to be more passive than active)

- Environmental barriers (e.g. mobility problems, living far away from supportive friends and family members, etc.)

You can let the patient know that many people with MS have noticed that there are two things that get in the way of receiving the support they need: (1) being socially isolated, and (2) having difficulty asking for support.

Decreasing Isolation

Explain that isolation is one of the most difficult problems people can face, because having emotional and social support is so critical to our well-being. Without support, people can sink into depression. We lose our motivation to try to improve our world. We begin to see things as hopeless. Isolation is clear from the People in My Life form when there is a dearth of people.

Decreasing isolation takes a concerted effort, and involves multiple strategies. Following are some examples:

1. Identify the reason for isolation or obstacles to interacting with others. Is isolation due to physical limitations (e.g. fatigue or other symptoms)? How much of it is caused by negative thinking patterns that discourage the patient from taking action to decrease her isolation (e.g. nobody will want to talk with me)?

2. If belief obstacles get in the way, evaluate negative thinking using the tools from chapters 6 and 7. You may wish to work together with the patient to complete an Unhelpful Thought Diary to examine her thoughts about initiating social contact or interacting with others in a social setting.

3. A possible strategy for helping the patient increase social interactions might involve identifying places to meet people, such as:

   - Community or neighborhood associations
   - Civic participation (e.g. towns and cities usually have advisory panels for everything from architectural preservation to health services. These panels are made up of volunteering citizens)
   - Advocacy or political activities (political parties, organizations that promote specific causes)
   - Classes or lectures
   - Church, synagogue, or other place of worship
   - Labor union
   - Business or professional groups
   - Support groups
   - Book clubs
   - Numerous Internet sites provide ways for people who have similar interests to meet. At the time of this writing, one such site is www.meetup.com.
   - Other: Ask the patient if she has any ideas.

Therapist Note

■ *Emphasize that it is best to choose an organization or activity that is meaningful to the patient. Since it usually takes a while to start meeting people, it is important that the activity is meaningful to the patient even while she is not meeting people.* ■

4. Using the People in My Life worksheet in the workbook, encourage the patient to take a look to see if she has friends or acquaintances with whom she has not had much social contact. Look at ways of using the existing relationships to bolster the social support network.

5. Help the patient plan these activities. Use the principles learned in chapter 3 on activity scheduling and apply them to activities focused on enhancing social interactions.

6. Evaluate if the patient maintains her social network. Emphasize that developing a social support network is not something you can do overnight. And, support networks need to be maintained.

Asking for Support

Try to help patients distinguish between their own discomfort at asking for or wanting support and the actual availability. To do this, you can review the People in My Life form and ask the patient the following:

■ "When was the last time you asked each of the people listed for that type of support?"

■ "How comfortable or uncomfortable was it?"

■ If the patient has not asked for support in a while, ask "How comfortable do you think you would be asking for that type of support from each individual?" (It is best if you can first determine something the patient could foresee asking for help with.)

Review some strategies for patients to consider that can help them overcome barriers to asking for support:

1. Use an Unhelpful Thought Diary to examine thoughts that interfere with asking for support. Often these thoughts involve

concern about the reactions of others, the perceptions of others, and self-image (e.g. what the patient tells herself about herself).

2. Develop ways of challenging these thoughts. Social cognitions can be very entrenched. Challenging the thoughts is critical. If possible, help the patient view the thoughts as tests to be tested behaviorally.

   - Identify a person and a request that are:
     Not overly anxiety-provoking or intimidating
     Likely to result in a positive response
   - Verify that the person is a good candidate for providing that form of support.
   - Do a thought record around fears (or assign thought record to complete prior to the request).
   - Ask the patient what success would look like. Help the patient define success in terms of how she makes the request, and not what the person's answer is. Making a good request that is rejected should be considered a success (even if it is possibly disappointing).

3. Have the patient watch and record her thoughts and feelings while receiving support (either requested or not requested).

4. Remind the patient to give positive feedback. Letting people know how much their help, friendship, or care means is both gratifying and reinforcing. Knowing that their help or support is appreciated helps people feel better and will make the patient feel better.

5. Suggest the patient request time from friends and family for *both* help-related activities and pleasure-related activities.

6. Brainstorm with the patient about new avenues for expressing feelings and receiving support (e.g. support groups, keeping a journal, enjoying time with pets, etc.).

Therapist Note

■ *Some people who report low levels of social support also have difficulties asserting themselves. This can leave the patient dissatisfied and sometimes resentful in relationships, which results in withdrawal and loneliness. Module 1 on communication and assertiveness may be useful for such individuals, along with continued focus on unhelpful thoughts that lead to avoidance.* ■

Your Ability to Provide Care and Support to Others

A growing literature is finding that when people help others, they are happier themselves (Schwartz & Sendor, 1999). Discuss with the patient that support is reciprocal. Providing support to others may be a rapid method of feeling more connected and building a sense of importance in our social environment. One of the most effective ways to improve one's own well-being and health is to help others.

When discussing the support the patient provides to people in her life or community, there are some important things to consider. First of all, support does not have to be returned in kind. For example, for someone who has a lot of physical impairments, it may be harder to provide practical support. But that person could just as easily provide emotional support. If a patient worries about being "needy" or a burden on her support system, she may want to talk with those individuals about how she either already does or could provide them with support.

Your Community

Talk with the patient about finding ways to do things for people in her community as one way to give to others (e.g. becoming involved in a church, synagogue, or place of worship, volunteering at a local MS society, or teaching people to read through a local library). You may want to say something like the following:

> *Giving to others helps people feel more connected, useful, and satisfied with their lives. This idea is an important one; keep it in mind not*

*only when you are providing support, but also when others are
providing support to you!*

Evaluating the Support the Patient Provides

Have the patient complete The Support I Provide form in the workbook
to help examine how she is providing support to those around her and
in her community. The form is similar to the one the patient completed
earlier examining the support that she receives. This time the patient
identifies for whom she provides the various types of support, and how
satisfying she finds that to be. Remind the patient that support is often
not reciprocal and we're not trying to see if things are "fair." The goal is
to look at the support she provides because providing support is good
for her.

For many patients, the exercise will serve primarily to highlight how she
also cares for others. Often there may be small things people can do that
greatly increase the sense that they are helpful to others (e.g. making a
little more effort to do something nice for a spouse, calling a friend or
family member a little more often, offering a small bit of assistance to a
neighbor, etc.). For patients who are more isolated, this can be a good
way to become more active socially. While there are traditional ways of
helping listed in the patient workbook (e.g. volunteering), encourage
the patient to also come up with her own ways of providing support to
the community or to friends and family.

Summary: How Social Support Fits in Our Stress and Mood Management Model

Review the model first presented in chapter 3 and this session's place
in it:

> *Our experience is made up of thoughts, feelings, physical sensations,
> behaviors, and social interactions. We have now begun working on
> the final part of the model: how your social world impacts or is
> impacted by your emotions, cognitions, behaviors, and physical
> responses.*

Homework

✎ Have the patient complete The People in My Life and The Support I Provide worksheets in the workbook. These forms include some of the concepts discussed in this chapter.

✎ For the isolated patient, encourage making one step toward decreasing that isolation, such as finding an activity, joining a club or group, signing up for a class, going to a church, synagogue, or place of worship, getting involved in a social, community, or political group, or by any other means.

✎ For the patient who has difficulty asking for help, encourage making a request for support in the coming week.

✎ Have the patient complete an Unhelpful Though Diary to see how thoughts and feelings affect and are affected by social interactions. Use the social interactions as the triggering events.

✎ If the patient is willing to consider providing support to others—either to individuals or through organizations—have the patient choose one person to do something for, or make a first phone call to volunteer at an organization.

✎ Have the patient select from among the optional modules in Part II of the workbook for review.

✎ Discuss any assignments relevant to the patient's goals.

Optional Treatment Modules

Module 1 *Communication and Assertiveness*

(Corresponds to chapter 7 of the workbook)

Materials Needed

- Copy of patient workbook
- DESC Exercise worksheet
- Unhelpful Thought Diary

Outline

- Set the agenda
- Rate the patient's stress/distress level
- Review homework
- Introduce communication skills
- Present styles of communication
- Review components of communication: active listening and express
- Teach the patient how to effectively respond to requests and steps for saying "no"
- Address beliefs and fears that act as obstacles to self-assertion
- Teach the patient how to effectively make complaints and requests
- Discuss how to deal with disappointment
- Assign homework

Set Agenda, Obtain Stress Rating, and Review Homework

Begin the session in the usual fashion, by setting the agenda and evaluating the patient's stress or distress over the previous week. Review the homework assigned in the previous session.

Therapist Note

■ *This module introduces patients to the idea that communication skills are important to overall well-being. It is primarily focused on assertiveness training, but also offers the opportunity to work on listening skills, if this is a problem. This module frequently requires several weeks of work or more. In randomized controlled trials of this treatment, this module has been among the most frequently selected (Mohr, Boudewyn, Goodkin, Bostrom, & Epstein, 2001; Mohr, Likosky et al., 2000; Mohr et al., 2005).* ■

Improving Communication Skills

Begin by telling the patient that almost everyone has difficulties with communication from time to time, particularly when there are conflicting needs or desires. First evaluate the types of problems the patient believes he has. This can include very general questions about what types of conversations are difficult or that the patient avoids. Is it hard to say no, and if so, under what circumstances? Is it hard to initiate conversations in which the patient is complaining about something or asking for something? Obtain a detailed description of recent situations including:

1. The type of situation

2. The patient's thoughts before any discussion and afterward. If the patient avoided discussion with the person, what were the thoughts about the avoidance?

3. The consequences of the behavior

Sometimes MS can further aggravate communication problems, particularly around assertiveness. Ask the patient if this is the case. Listen for issues around:

■ embarrassment or worry around other people's reactions to related MS

- changes in social roles as a result of MS—particularly when these changes are related to a loss of confidence

If any MS-related themes are present, follow up with these themes in the subsequent exercises and discussions.

There are certain skills patients can learn to become more assertive and better cope with daily challenges. In this section, patients will have the opportunity to:

1. Identify the four primary styles of communication, including their own

2. Identify beliefs they hold that maintain their unhelpful communication behaviors and barriers that interfere with effective communication

3. Practice specific communication skills

Styles of Communication

Present the four basic communication styles: passive, assertive, passive-aggressive, and aggressive. Explain that the style of communication we choose is usually a result of our beliefs about the importance of our needs compared to the needs of others.

Have the patient describe times when he used each communication style, and what the consequences were. If the patient is unable to generate times when he used a type of communication, you might also have him identify his experience when other people have used these types of communication.

As you discuss these different styles in more detail, ask the patient to try to think of which style he uses most often. Some people may be pretty uniform in the styles they use under difficult social circumstances. Other people may use different communication styles under different circumstances—at work versus with a partner, for example. Following are the descriptions from the patient workbook of each communication style.

Passive Communication

Passive communication puts the respect for the rights and needs of others above your own. Passive communication means that you tend to keep your thoughts and opinions to yourself. You are likely to say nothing (or little) when something bothers you. You may also have difficulty identifying and saying what you need or want.

Aggressive Communication

Aggressive communication is at the other extreme; it puts your rights above those of the listener. It means you tend to focus on "getting your way" or "having your say" rather than respecting the concerns of the other person or helping them understand your concerns.

Passive-Aggressive Communication

Passive-aggressive communication is sometimes used when a person is angry and wants to be aggressive, but also wants to avoid direct confrontation. This means you do something that will cause irritation in the other person, but in a way that leaves a plausible excuse. Common examples are being late and making people wait, not following through on things you promise to do, and so on. This type of communication can be particularly destructive because it aggravates the other person, while also shutting down avenues toward resolution. Neither your needs nor the needs of the other party are respected when communicating in a passive-aggressive manner.

Assertive Communication

Assertive communication is a more balanced and adaptive way of communicating. It balances respect for both yourself and the listener, and considers both your needs and the needs of the other person. Assertive communication allows you to express your needs or wants, but acknowledges that the other person's needs or wants may be different.

Continuum of Communication Styles

Many patients will express concern that their behavior is too passive or too aggressive. Often, when introduced to the Communication Continuum, patients express relief upon learning that they have other options for communication.

Explain that communication styles exist on a continuum from passive to aggressive, with assertive communication falling in the middle. Passive-aggressive communication is a combination of passive and aggressive communication styles, and does not fall on the continuum. Summarize the main characteristics of each style (see Figure M1.1).

Review with the patient whose needs are met with each of the four communication styles (see Table M1.1).

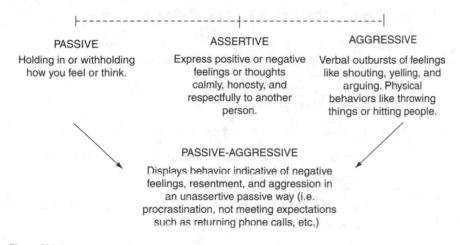

Figure M1.1
The Communication Continuum.

Table M1.1 Communication styles and needs met

Communication style	Your needs met?	Other's needs met?
Passive	No	Yes
Aggressive	Yes	No
Passive-Aggressive	No	No
Assertive	Yes	Yes

Emphasize that assertive communication is usually the most effective communication style. Note that there may be times when passive or aggressive communication is appropriate. For example, in an emergency situation, aggressive communication might be most efficient. But nine times out of ten, assertiveness is the best option.

Next, take a look more specifically at the components of effective communication.

Components of Communication: Active Listening and Expressing

Inform the patient that active listening and expressing are the main components of effective communication. If one person in a conversation or discussion is not listening or speaking clearly, it is like static on a telephone line—the communication breaks down. Listening and speaking are equally important for effective communication.

Active Listening

Active listening involves:

- focusing on understanding what the other person is saying.

- making sure you accurately understand what the other person has said.

- letting the other person know that you've understood what he has said.

In summarizing, tell the patient that when listening actively, we make sure that we accurately understand the other person while letting the person know that we understand. There are a variety of different techniques we can use to let the other person know that we have heard and understood what he has said. One way is to paraphrase and repeat back what the other person has said to ensure that we understand it correctly and let the other person know that we've understood.

You may want to say something like the following:

> *Most people do not actively listen during conversations. Instead of intently focusing on hearing and understanding the other person, it is*

common for people to think about what to say next, to anticipate what the other person will say next, or even to drift off and think about something completely unrelated. When we do these things, it is like mental static that interferes with our listening. In these situations we are more likely to hear what we expect to hear, rather than what we actually hear. When others perceive that we are not really listening and hearing their concerns, they often feel frustrated, resentful, and dissatisfied with the interaction. As a result, they may withdraw or complain. On the other hand, when others feel really listened to and understood, they feel cared for and are more likely to actively listen to us. Active listening is an important component of providing support to others.

Explain that active listening is a skill that can be applied to many different situations. It can:

■ be an important component of letting others know that you care about them.

■ be used in situations in which there is a high potential for conflict (including when you are responding to a request made of you or when you are making a request of another).

■ defuse potentially difficult interactions by allowing you to step back before reacting.

People who are more effective at managing conflict tend to be those who listen better. Emphasize that if we *really* listen to what the other person has to say, we are more likely to respond with compassion and empathy, even when disagreeing or saying no.

Active Listening Exercise

Review the patient's impression of his own active listening skills. The following questions may be helpful:

■ "What is it like for you when you listen to other people?"

■ "In general, do you feel you are a good listener? In what ways are you a good listener?"

- "What are some of the things that get in the way of your active listening? (Anticipating what the other person will say and interrupting? Anticipating your response? Being distracted? Daydreaming? Other?)"

- "What are some of the consequences of not actively or accurately listening or understanding someone? Can you think of specific examples? What about the results when you have actively listened?"

Of particular importance is identifying what gets in the way of active listening. If the patient says nothing gets in the way, push a little bit.

- Is the patient able to listen just as well when he is anxious? Angry? Impatient?

- Is the patient able to listen when the other person is boring, antagonistic, or angry?

- What does the patient do in these instances? Daydream? Anticipate what the other person will say? Finish sentences? Stop listening?

- How can the patient do a better job of listening under these circumstances?

Styles of Expression

Stress that listening is only one side of the communication equation. Effective communication also requires effective expression. However, many people think the goal of talking is "to say what I need to say" Or "to tell someone something." Point out to the patient that this goal does not involve the listener. Communication is, by definition, a two-way street. The goal of expressing ourselves is to help others understand and respond to our needs.

Review the four styles of expressing, each of which corresponds to one of the communication styles. During this review, ask the patient to try to think of the style that best describes how he expresses himself.

Monologue

Some people tend to dominate a conversation and give others little airtime. This style of expressing is most common in *aggressive communication*. To improve expression skills in this case, the challenge will involve talking less and listening more. Being concise helps the other person to listen better to what you have to say.

Too Shy to Speak

Some people tend to hesitate before expressing themselves because they consider their thoughts or needs to be unimportant, or because they fear being criticized by others. This style of expressing is most common in *passive communication*. To improve expression skills in this case, the challenge will be to speak up and worry less about how you might be perceived.

Confusing Speech

Some people communicate their needs indirectly, and may even be hesitant to acknowledge their needs to others. They may phrase their needs in a cryptic manner, making it difficult or even impossible for the listener to understand. This style of expressing is most common in *passive-aggressive communication*. The challenge for you in this case is to clearly state your needs, and worry less about how you might be perceived.

Dialogue

Some people are good at balancing their expressing with listening, which allows for a productive verbal exchange. This style of expressing is most common in *assertive communication*. In this case, communication is more effective because both parties express their ideas and are willing to listen to each other.

Expression Style Exercise

Of course, how we deal with difficult conversations varies with the topic and with whom we are speaking. For example, a person might be very assertive or aggressive with a family member, but passive with conflict in the work place. You might want to have the patient do the following exercise for several situations.

Have the patient think back to the last time he had had a difficult conversation or avoided a difficult conversation. This might have been when he said "no" to a request (or wanted to, but could not say "no") or when he needed to raise a difficult topic with someone (e.g. talking to someone about something they are doing that bothers him, or raising a difficult topic with a boss). Ask the following questions:

- "What was the situation?"

- "What did you say?"

- "What difficulties did you have in responding to this request? For example, did you have trouble saying 'no?' Did you have any negative feelings come up, like anger or guilt?"

- "How would you describe your communication style, particularly during difficult or conflictual conversation?"

- "How would you describe your expressive style?"

- "If you did not use assertive communication or dialogue, what do you think it would have been like for you to use these?"

Obstacles to Self-Assertion: Beliefs and Fears

Many of us develop different beliefs or even fears around self-assertion. Have the patient think back over his life. What kind of response did he receive to needs, requests, and assertions? Where did he not assert himself, or have difficulties asserting himself effectively? What were some of the beliefs, thoughts, or fears that got in the way or prevented him from communicating assertively?

Review with the patient the following list of underlying fears or beliefs he may have experienced when he asserted himself. The same list is provided in the workbook.

- Fear of not being loved or liked

- Fear of being rejected

- Fear of hurting the other person's feelings

- Fear of being put down or feeling humiliated

- Fear of making a mess

- Fear of being ignored

- Fear of becoming violent or inappropriately angry

- Fear of looking bad (e.g. looking stupid, weak, crazy, or greedy)

- Fear of being seen as not masculine/feminine

- Fear of being hurt if told "No"

- Fear of being laughed at

- Fear of not being respected

Remind patients that this list is not exhaustive and is just meant to be used as a tool to help them become more aware.

Becoming More Assertive

Review how to handle two difficult types of communications. One is saying "no" to a request when feeling pressured to say "yes." The other is making requests and complaints when we anticipate that the other person will not be happy with us. Inform the patient that the key components of each strategy are to foster good communication by expressing thoughts and feelings in a way that helps the other person understand us and our position, listening effectively and letting the other person know that we are listening by paraphrasing, repeating what we understand,

and asking questions to clarify our understanding, and by not backing down quickly or unreasonably.

Saying "No" and Responding to Other's Requests

Responding to requests from others can feel challenging when what others are asking of us conflicts with our needs. Let the patient know that this can be uncomfortable for most of us. However, there are some basic skills that the patient can use to communicate his needs, even in difficult or potentially confrontational situations. Review the following steps.

The Five Steps to Saying "No"

Step 1: Acknowledge the other person's request, even if you know you cannot satisfy the request.

Example: (Friend's request to take care of the dog while he is away). *I completely understand that you need someone to take care of your dog.*

Step 2: State your situation, wishes, needs, and your position. Postponing a difficult discussion often just makes it worse.

Example: *Between work and the kids, I am already feeling pretty overloaded. It would be very hard to find the time to get in the car to come over and take care of the dog every day.*

Step 3: Listen to the other person, even if what he has to say is difficult to hear.

Step 4: Let the other person know you understand what he is saying. Respond to the request nonjudgmentally and with empathy. Speaking with empathy will make the other person feel heard and understood.

Example: *I understand that your dog is more comfortable with me, and of course you want what is best for your dog. And I like your dog.*

Step 5: Restate your position, if appropriate. Offer alternatives if possible.

Example: *I am sorry, but I am just too overwhelmed. Isn't there a neighbor who can at least feed the dog?*

Therapist Note

■ *Often patients who are passive or easily influenced will quickly feel like they are in the wrong. Aggressive patients may quickly become irritated. Suggest that patients watch for these signs when practicing assertiveness. Let them know that it will feel uncomfortable not to reply to requests in their characteristic manner. One way of managing this is to remind them that they can ask for time to think about the request—it is usually not imperative to answer right away. This will allow them time to think through the request and to practice responding assertively.* ■

Role Play

Practicing with the patient is a critical step to helping him learn the skills and gain sufficient confidence to be able to implement the skills successfully. Have the patient identify examples of when he wanted to say no but didn't. You will play the role of the person making the request. The first time through, help the patient think through what he will say in advance. Then, proceed with the role play. Do as many role plays as necessary to help the patient be comfortable. You may need to continue doing these role plays over the course of several sessions.

Making Complaints and Requests

Reiterate that good communication depends both on expressing our thoughts and feelings in a way that helps the other person understand us and our position and on our ability to listen effectively. In the next section, patients will learn specific skills that will help them improve their general expressiveness and assertiveness. One such strategy is called the DESC model (Bower & Bower, 1991), which can be useful both in expressing complaints and in making requests to others. You may introduce the model by saying something like the following:

> *For a lot of people, making requests or complaints is uncomfortable. It can be difficult to bring up conversations that may create conflict. There may be a number of ways to effectively make these kinds of*

communications. It is helpful to have a simple strategy for making complaints or requests when you find yourself uncomfortable, either because of anxiety or because of anger.

Introduce the DESC method as one that is relatively simple and effective. The steps are as follows:

D: Describe

E: Express

S: Specific changes

C: Consequences (positive) of the request

The first two steps are useful in providing criticisms. Using all four steps provides a basic strategy for making requests. If the patient finds it difficult to make requests or provide others with feedback, use an Unhelpful Thought Diary (UTD) to help him understand why it is hard for him.

Review the specifics of each step as follows:

D: Describe

Describe the complaint or request. Think carefully about what you want to say or ask. It is important to be able to describe what you want to say or ask as clearly as possible. This requires that you be clear about what you want to communicate before you begin to talk with another person. When you are ready to describe what you want to say or ask, be sure to describe your thinking about the request or complaint in a direct and nonjudgmental manner. (See examples in the workbook).

E: Express

Express how you feel. When expressing your feelings, it is best to be direct, open, and use "I" statements such as "I feel scared of..." or "I feel hurt when..." or "I felt frustrated when you forget to...."

Using "I" statements is an important communication tool that helps create a more collaborative and less judgmental interaction. Think about how different it sounds to say "I feel angry when . . ." versus "You make me so mad when you . . ." In the first example, the same emotion (anger) is conveyed, but without the judgment. This makes it easier for the other person to respond without feeling defensive, and opens the door to a more clear communication process.

S: Specific Changes

Ask for *specific changes*. The more specific and clear you can be about what you want, the more likely you are to be satisfied with the outcome. For instance, saying "I'd like you to call me back within 3 days after I call you" is more specific than "You need to be better about showing me you care about me." The latter may still be true, but it is not specific enough, and doesn't provide enough guidance for the other person.

C: Consequences (positive)

Think through the *consequences* of making your request. It is best to frame the consequences positively—the effect if the person agrees with you. Negative consequences (what will happen if you *don't* get what you want) can be heard as a threat, and can increase tension. Stating the positive consequences of what will happen if the other person does what you want is more of an incentive.

Emphasize that no matter what the outcome, the goal of assertive communication is to communicate our wants and needs in a respectful manner. The other person retains the right to not meet our request.

Role Playing the DESC Exercise

After explaining the DESC model, have the patient identify several recent or anticipated problems involving interpersonal conflict that might be addressed through more assertive behavior (because of overly passive, aggressive, or passive-aggressive responses). You will need to identify a couple of these problems to work on in the session, and potentially one problem to address in homework, if the patient feels ready. To select problems, have the patient rate how strong his emotional response is (usually anxiety or anger). Select problems that are of moderate intensity—enough emotion to be a problem, but not enough to be overwhelming.

For the first problem, go through the DESC Exercise in the workbook with the patient. Help the patient think through exactly how to **describe** the problem, **express** the feeling(s), ask for **specific changes**, and describe the positive **consequences** of this change (Note that the consequences should be positive, and not threats). Also be sure you understand enough about the person the patient would use the DESC method with so that you can accurately play him in a role play. That is, what are the behaviors that the patient is afraid of, worried about, or might be triggers?

Once you have coached the patient and you understand your character in the role play, engage in a role play using those materials. Also be sure to incorporate some of the threats to listening that the patient identified earlier. Following the role play, discuss how it went, how the patient is feeling, what thoughts he has, etc. Be alert to thoughts that he will not be able to do this in real life. Go through additional role plays, practicing and following up on thoughts and feelings.

Encourage the patient to generate a list, during the session, of people, places, and situations, in which assertiveness skills are likely to be most beneficial. As many patients indicate that they wish to be more assertive in interactions with their doctors, it may be helpful to ask about the patient's level of physician/patient communications.

Therapist Note

■ *Moderate the patient's expectations. It should be clear to the patient that assertive communication does NOT mean that he will get what he wants. It means that both he and the other person will be able to discuss the issues. Assertiveness increases the likelihood that some sort of compromise will be found, but it does not guarantee it. The goal of this caveat is to uncouple success in being assertive from success in getting what is wanted. Thus, the patient can have a successful experience if he expresses himself in an assertive manner, even if the conflict is not resolved in his favor.* ■

Evaluating Communication

Changing old habits is very hard. Tell the patient that it is helpful to think of this as a project in "continuing self-improvement." When the patient has had an encounter in which he engaged in, or could have engaged in assertive behavior, he should go back and first look at what he did well, and then see if there is anything to learn. Questions to ask include:

- ■ "What worked, and what did you do well?"

- ■ "What things might you do better the next time?"

- ■ "Did the other person understand what you were saying? If not, was there anything you could have done to make it more likely the other person would understand?"

- ■ "Did you understand what the other person was saying, and if not, was there anything you could have done differently?"

Encourage patients to give themselves credit for using their communication skills, and for taking an interpersonal risk and trying new behaviors, regardless of how well they did and regardless of the outcome.

Dealing with Disappointment

The purpose of this module has been to help patients express their needs and wants in a manner that encourages discussion. Let patients know that while this may increase the likelihood that they will be more successful in these kinds of interactions, using these techniques cannot guarantee that they will always get what they want. Even when we have used assertive communication, listened to others, and used the DESC method, there is always the possibility that the person we are talking to will not agree with us, or may even react in ways that are unhelpful.

This can be disappointing. However, patients have learned a lot of techniques that can be helpful in managing disappointment, some of which are listed in the workbook.

Homework

The goal is to incorporate these behaviors into the patient's life. However, some people are not ready for such an assignment after the first session. In these cases, it may be best to have interim goals. For example:

✎ Have the patient find a time to use the new communication skills introduced this week (active listening, saying no, making a request or complaint using the DESC method). He should keep track of how these techniques work for him and any results or consequences from this new mode of communicating.

✎ If the patient has difficulty with the techniques, instruct him to identify conflictual situations and complete an Unhelpful Thought Diary or DESC exercise on paper.

✎ Have the patient continue to keep a UTD to see how his thoughts and feelings affect and are affected by his social interactions. He should use social interactions as the triggering events, paying special attention to times when he either wants to assert himself or does (this can include responding to requests or making requests as well). The patient should come prepared next session to talk about thought patterns he may have noticed. Also, it is important that the patient fill out this form as completely as he can, but let him know it is okay if he cannot fill out all the columns.

✎ Assign reading in the workbook as appropriate.

✎ Discuss any assignments relevant to the patient's goals.

Module 2   *Fatigue and Energy Conservation*

(Corresponds to chapter 8 of the workbook)

Materials Needed

- Copy of patient workbook
- Fatigue Diary
- Pacing Activities Worksheet
- Fatigue Goal Worksheet

Outline

- Set the agenda
- Rate the patient's stress/distress level
- Review homework
- Identify potential sources of fatigue
- Present the three A's in learning how to cope with fatigue
- Discuss additional strategies for managing MS fatigue
- Help the patient set goals related to fatigue
- Assign homework

Therapist Note

- *As with most of these modules, teaching fatigue management may take several sessions.*

Set Agenda, Obtain Stress Rating, and Review Homework

Begin the session in the usual fashion, by setting the agenda and evaluating the patient's stress or distress over the previous week. Review the homework assigned in the previous session.

Understanding MS Fatigue

Fatigue is the most common problem in MS, with up to 90% of patients experiencing some tiredness (Freal, Kraft, & Coryell, 1984) and for many it is their most debilitating symptom (Fisk, Pontefract, Ritvo, Archibald, & Murray, 1994). The etiology of fatigue in MS is poorly understood. It is a "non-specific" symptom, and likely has many causes. The goal of this module is to help patients identify patterns of fatigue, potential sources of fatigue, and to come up with methods of managing fatigue.

Fatigue is difficult to treat effectively. A few medications exist that are partially effective in reducing fatigue severity. However, even when these medications are helpful, they do not "cure" the problem. As with many MS symptoms, learning how to manage fatigue can make a big difference in the patient's quality of life.

Begin working with a brief evaluation of the patient's fatigue. Some patients can talk at great length about fatigue, given how potentially disabling it can be. Try to limit this evaluation to 5–10 min by reassuring the patient that you will be going into great detail to understand her fatigue. Some initial things to ask include:

1. How severe is the fatigue, when is it worst (typically this is the afternoons), and what brings it on or makes it worse?

2. How does the fatigue affect the patient's ability to do things?

3. What efforts has the patient made to manage the fatigue and how successful have those efforts been?

4. Has the patient discussed fatigue with her neurologist or doctor, and if so, when and what was discussed? If the patient has not

discussed fatigue with her doctor in more than a year, suggest that she do so. Nevertheless, you can begin with this module.

5.   What medications, if any, is the patient taking for fatigue?

Next, describe what the fatigue module entails. First, you will review the different types of fatigue. Then you will describe the need to assess, or keep track of fatigue. Then, in the coming weeks, you will use that information to understand the source and impact of the fatigue better and to come up with better ways to manage it.

Help the patient have reasonable expectations. The goal is to better manage the fatigue—this will not eliminate fatigue. But if successful, the strategies in this module should help the patient experience less fatigue and possibly be more active.

Types of Fatigue

Go through each of the following types of fatigue with the patient and ask if she experiences any of them. If a particular type of fatigue is a problem, elicit a concrete example from the patient (do not talk about fatigue in the abstract). Explore with the patient what led up to the fatigue, what the consequences were, how she managed it, and, if appropriate, what cognitions were involved.

In listening to the patient, assess for overaccommodation or underaccommodation (or assimilation).

Overaccommodation is when the patient's attempts to accommodate are more extensive than required by the fatigue, and result in unnecessary restrictions in the fulfillment of roles and participation in activities. For example, a runner who begins to have some fatigue and decides to stop exercising in general may be overaccommodating.

Underaccommodation occurs when the patient does not make adequate changes in behavior or activities to adjust to fatigue (or any other symptom). Typically these patients are "fighters" and somewhat proud of this trait. However, underaccommodation can be physically dangerous, because patients will continue engaging in activities that their bodies can no longer support. For example, patients who underaccommodate fatigue may be more likely to experience falls.

If underaccommodation or overaccommodation are present, more cognitive work will likely be required to examine the underlying cognitions driving these maladaptive strategies.

Normal Fatigue

This is the type of fatigue that everyone experiences from time to time. Physical, mental, and emotional exertion makes everyone tired. There's nothing necessarily bad about this type of fatigue, and it resolves easily with rest.

Fatigue from Depression and Stress

Fatigue can result from depression or feeling distressed. This kind of fatigue is often about not feeling interested in doing things or motivated to do things; it is being tired *of* things, rather than tired *from* things. If a person feels uninterested in doing anything, it might be related to depression. Usually when a person feels fatigued, either from normal fatigue or fatigue resulting from MS, rest usually improves the condition. However, for depression-related fatigue, rest can make it worse. When depression and distress are effectively treated, symptoms of fatigue often improve.

Disability Fatigue

This is the type of fatigue that results from compensating for disabilities. The effects of MS on muscle control, coordination, and strength can result in a person expending more effort to accomplish routine tasks. For example, if a person has difficulty walking because of spasticity, then walking will likely take more energy, thereby increasing fatigue.

Deconditioning Fatigue

Deconditioning takes place when muscle strength is poor because muscles have not been used for a period of time. If a person has fatigue because of deconditioning, she may find that her muscles weaken quickly after having used them for only a short time. For deconditioning fatigue, brief rest usually restores some of the strength/energy. People who have increased weakness, heat sensitivity, and fatigue can easily be caught in a vicious cycle in which less activity leads to loss of muscle strength, which leads to less activity and more weakness, and worse fatigue, and so on.

Fatigue from Sleep Disturbance

MS symptoms such as bladder problems, spasticity, pain, random tingling, burning, numb sensations, and even some medications can all interfere with restful sleep, sometimes even without a person's awareness. A person may notice herself waking up frequently at night because of any of these problems. Or, a person may find that she does not feel rested even after a full night of sleep. If so, sleep disturbance may be one source of fatigue.

Heat-Related Fatigue

For people with MS, fatigue is related to heat. A person will notice heat fatigue if fatigue increases as the ambient temperature increases (as in summer) or if body temperature increases (e.g. through exertion or through fever). It is believed that heat causes fatigue by slowing the conduction of the electrical impulses down the axon.

Fatigue from Diet Problems

While no diets have been shown to be good for MS specifically, it is important to have a healthy balanced diet. High sugar and low carbohydrate intake, as well as some fad diets, can increase fatigue. Alcohol and cigarette use can also substantially worsen fatigue. Overeating can also increase fatigue. Ultimately, as there is no scientific evidence that MS has a dietary cause or cure, there is no need for a special diet. A nutritious, well-balanced diet (the one recommended for most people) is also most likely the best for individuals with MS.

Although diet-related fatigue is not analyzed in this module, tell patients that it is a good idea to try to maintain a healthy diet. Tracking one's diet can help pinpoint any nutritional deficits that may be contributing to poor energy. If this is something the patient would like to do, discuss it further and work it into her goals. There are also numerous good books on healthy eating and lifestyle. One geared toward people with MS is Susan Epstein's *The LIFE Program for MS: Lifestyle, Independence, Fitness, and Energy.*

Primary MS Fatigue

Although little is known about MS fatigue, there are many ideas about the causes. One hypothesis is that it is related to *demyelination*. Demyelination is the destructive removal of myelin, an insulating and protective fatty protein that sheaths nerve cells (neurons). As the myelin sheath is destroyed, the axon is less efficient at conducting electrical impulses. These electrical impulses are how nerves communicate with each other. When these impulses are slowed or weakened, it may translate into a person being slowed, weakened, or fatigued. Another hypothesis is that MS inflammation triggers the brain to produce hormones that can increase fatigue and feelings of distress.

Whatever the cause is, primary MS fatigue tends to occur daily, and often worsens as the day progresses, reaching its height in the afternoon. It can be aggravated by many of the factors that in and of themselves also contribute to fatigue in MS, such as heat, humidity, depression, stress, deconditioning, and sleep problems. Primary MS fatigue can come on suddenly. For example, a person who typically has no trouble walking across a room may develop a limp after walking a block, and may be close to collapse after three or four blocks. Primary MS fatigue is qualitatively different from normal fatigue. It is difficult to describe to people who have not experienced it. But if a patient has experienced it, it should be readily identifiable.

Three A's for Coping with Fatigue

Present to the patient the three A's in learning how to cope with fatigue:

Assess: The patient will carefully evaluate her activity and level of fatigue throughout the day for approximately 1 week.

Analyze: You and the patient will review the information collected to look for patterns, and to try to understand what might be contributing to the fatigue. Based on this information the two of you will come up with possible solutions.

Act: Then the patient will be able to try out the solutions. Some of the solutions may be helpful and some may not. The patient can continue assessing and evaluating the fatigue until a reasonably satisfactory method of managing the fatigue is found.

Assessing Fatigue

Explain that the first step is to try to understand the patient's fatigue better by *assessing* when, why, and how it occurs—times of the day when it is worse, the conditions that bring it on (e.g. heat), and so on. The patient may have some ideas about these things, but a thorough assessment can reveal other valuable patterns and information that can improve coping with fatigue. The Fatigue Diary, which the patient will keep for 1 week, provides the basis of this assessment.

The Fatigue Diary should be introduced during the first week of fatigue work. Complete a Fatigue Diary with the patient in the session for that day. If the appointment is in the early morning, complete it for the previous day. In completing this diary, ask the patient to document activities several times throughout the day. She will also be asked to rate her level of fatigue, the importance of the activity, and the satisfaction derived from this activity. By documenting each of these things, the patient will be able to identify the sources of fatigue, as well as possible solutions. In addition, at the end of each day, the patient should rate how much fatigue interfered with her ability to do things. Once the solutions have been implemented, the level of fatigue should continue to be monitored to judge their effectiveness. See Figure 8.1 in the workbook for an example of a completed Fatigue Diary.

Assign the Fatigue Diary as homework for the first week. With the patient, identify a time of day, and a place where it will be completed. The following week, when the patient comes with the completed diary, you and the patient can begin analyzing the information in the diary.

Analyzing Fatigue

After completing the Fatigue Diary for 5–7 days, the patient will be ready to *analyze* her fatigue and begin coming up with solutions. First help the patient reflect on the activities she recorded on her Fatigue Diary. Has the patient noticed any patterns? Are there specific activities that seem to be more fatiguing? Times of the day? Are there things that make it better? What types of fatigue are most prominent?

Look at the importance of each activity, the level of satisfaction with each activity, and the different types of fatigue the patient experiences during and after each activity.

- Are there activities that have low importance and low satisfaction that can be eliminated?

- Sometimes people feel some activities are more important than they are. Are there unsatisfying activities for which the patient may be overestimating the importance?

- Can the frequency or length of activities be shortened?

- Are there activities that can be done by someone else? For example, does the patient have the ability to hire a cleaning person? Can groceries be delivered (many communities have stores that allow online purchasing and delivery)?

- Are there places where putting in breaks would help preserve energy?

- Can duties be rearranged? For example, if a person is doing activities outside in the afternoon during the heat of summer, those activities might be better scheduled for the early morning.

- Ask the patient if she absolutely had to drop three (or whatever number) activities from her schedule, which three would they be?

- Help the patient come up with other creative solutions. Often people, once confronted with the information from their Fatigue Dairies, are very creative in coming up with solutions.

Acting to Reduce Fatigue

Once the various sources of the patient's fatigue have been analyzed, turn to what can be done to cope with each type of fatigue. Take notes about what the patient identifies may be helpful.

Normal Fatigue

This is the easiest form of fatigue to cope with. We are trained all our lives to deal with this kind of fatigue. Usually a little rest will help.

Fatigue from Depression and Stress

The key to combating fatigue from depression and stress is to reduce the depression and stress. Thus, the same things that help depression should help this type of fatigue. Unlike most types of fatigue that improve with rest, rest can sometimes worsen depression-related fatigue. The way to combat this fatigue is to *do more*. Regardless of the source of the fatigue, a growing body of evidence shows that treatments for stress and depression reduce fatigue severity (Mohr, Hart, & Goldberg, 2003; Mohr, Hart, & Vella, 2007). The skills taught in this program—changing the way one thinks, scheduling pleasant activities, improving one's social support, and developing good coping habits—can improve fatigue.

Disability Fatigue

Disability fatigue is the fatigue that comes from the added effort required to do things from MS-related impairments (e.g. the extra energy it takes to walk if you have spasticity in your legs). Compensating, using mobility aids, and modifying the environment are all options for combating this type of fatigue. Present each of these strategies as follows:

Compensating. This strategy for dealing with disability fatigue is to limit one's reliance on the parts of one's body that do not work well, and increase reliance on the parts that do work well, particularly when trying to accomplish a task (exercise may be useful, as will be discussed later on). Tell the patient that a lot of people use the opposite strategy. That is, they find themselves having trouble with a leg or an arm, and they try to use it more. This leads only to frustration, and ultimately to cutting back on activities. Give the patient this rule of thumb: "If you are trying to get something done, do it the easy way. Life is hard enough. Why make it even harder?"

Mobility Aids. Mobility aids and energy-saving strategies can provide some relief from disability fatigue. Evaluate if the patient has difficulty walking (notice subtle gait problems when she walks). Be on the alert for falls, fatigue, or other signs that aids are required. If there are problems, urge the patient to see a physical therapist or an occupational therapist to review options for aids. These might include an ankle-foot orthosis (AFO), a cane, or other types of assistance.

Many people avoid getting mobility aids until long after they need them. This is sometimes because of anxiety. Often patients have thoughts or beliefs about mobility aids that typically include being worried about stigma or that they would be giving in to the disease. If the patient might benefit from aids, it can be helpful to talk further about these issues or work through a thought diary.

Modifying Environment. Patients may be able to modify their environments to minimize reliance on the body parts that are affected by MS and thus contribute to fatigue. Suggestions are provided in the workbook and include setting up an easy work flow, sitting down as much as possible when performing certain tasks (e.g. getting dressed), carrying objects in a bag or a cart instead of holding them in the hands, and setting up "workstations" around the house.

Deconditioning Fatigue

Deconditioning fatigue occurs when muscles have been weakened through lack of use. People who have increased weakness, heat sensitivity, and fatigue can easily be caught in a vicious cycle in which less activity leads to loss of muscle strength. This can lead to even less activity, more weakness, and worse fatigue.

The key to overcoming deconditioning fatigue is exercise. Patients are sometimes confused by the apparently contradictory recommendations to accommodate disabilities but exercise to avoid deconditioning. The emphasis is to compensate to allow people to do the things they want and need to do, but not to let that compensation lead to deconditioning. Admittedly this is a difficult balance to find. Done regularly over time, exercise will improve conditioning. Muscles that are regularly exercised grow more tolerant of activity. Emphasize that this means that exercise increases the amount the patient *can* do. There are other possible benefits of exercise, as well, including reduced spasticity, better sleep, better mood—all of which may further lessen fatigue.

Despite the many benefits of exercise, there are risks. Make sure the patient keeps in mind the guidelines presented in the workbook when starting an exercise program. These include speaking with a doctor first, exercising at a moderate intensity in a cool environment to avoid overheating, paying attention to the body's signals, and enlisting the help of a physical therapist if necessary.

Therapist Note

■ *Advise discretion in developing any exercise program. If the patient finds she is too tired to engage in normal activities after exercise, she may need to modify the activity (such as fewer repetitions, or shorter duration) or space the activity out more evenly during the day.* ■

There are several types of exercise, all of which may help manage fatigue. Review these with the patient:

Aerobic exercise: It is recommended that people with mild or moderate MS maintain aerobic fitness by doing something energetic enough to raise their pulse rate, three times a week. If the patient is able to jog or walk, that may be an option. For people with mobility or balance problems, a stationary bike may be a good alternative. Swimming is an excellent exercise, and the cool water is helpful for people who are heat sensitive.

Stretching exercises: Many people with MS have spasticity, especially in their lower extremities that can cause the legs to stiffen. A regular stretching program can help maintain or improve muscle length and allow flexibility. Stretching exercises are available on the National MS Society's Web site (www.nationalmssociety.org). More and more people with MS are exploring Tai Chi and Yoga as methods of maintaining flexibility.

Strengthening exercises: Strengthening exercises are designed to build weakened muscles and can aid in moving and walking. As mentioned earlier, patients should not overdo it. It is better to do less, or exercise briefly several times a day, than to exercise to the point of becoming fatigued.

Heat-Related Fatigue

Many people with MS are heat sensitive. That is, heat makes them even more tired.

The key to combating heat fatigue is to stay cool. Encourage the patient to observe the following tips:

- Use the air conditioner whenever possible, at home or in the car

- Use fans

- Take a cool shower

- Sit in a cool bath for 20 min (start with lukewarm water and slowly add cold water)

- Keep cold drinks handy (avoid sugared soda pop). You can also keep ice chips in your mouth.

- Cool off with a spray bottle or a wet towel

- Plan heavier activity for cooler parts of the day, preferably earlier

If a patient is especially heat sensitive, she may want to consider getting a cooling vest. Patients can talk to a neurologist or a physical therapist about this.

Fatigue Due to Sleep Problems

Problems with sleep can come from a variety of sources. Sometimes difficulty in sleeping is related to depression or anxiety. Many of the tools in the first chapters of this book should help patients learn to manage sleep problems more effectively.

Sometimes sleep difficulties are related to MS symptoms. Needing to get up during the night to use the bathroom is very common. Sometimes people also find they have muscle twitching or spasms, spasticity, pain, or other problems that can interfere with sleep. It may be useful for patients to talk with their doctors about what can be done to reduce these symptoms.

Prescription medications can have an effect on sleep, and patients should ask their physician or pharmacist about drowsiness or stimulation as a side effect of their medications. If a prescription drug makes a patient drowsy when she needs to perform at her peak, or hyperalert when she needs to sleep, have her consult with her doctor about adjusting the timing of the medication.

Even if the sleep problem is partly related to physical symptoms, there are often things we do that make it harder to sleep, and things we can do to improve sleep. Review some things a person can do that, over time, will likely improve sleep. These include going to bed at the same time every night, getting up at the same time every morning, avoiding naps, and refraining from drinking caffeinated drinks after noon. Patients should also avoid drinking alcohol late in the day and smoking cigarettes in general. More detailed "sleep rules" can be found in another book in the Treatments *ThatWork*™ series, *Over-coming Insomnia: A Cognitive-Behavioral Therapy Approach, Therapist Guide* (Edinger & Carney, 2008). This book outlines a safe and effective treatment that targets the behavioral and cognitive components of insomnia. The program focuses on educating the patient about sleep, addressing unhelpful beliefs about sleep, and teaching ways to eliminate sleep-disruptive habits.

Primary MS Fatigue

There are a few medications that may be helpful for primary MS fatigue. Modafinil (Provigil®), amantadine (Symetrel®), pemoline (Cylert®), and methylphenidate (Ritalin®) are the most widely prescribed. These medications can be helpful for many people, but even when beneficial, they usually do not completely eliminate fatigue. Next are a few additional strategies for managing MS fatigue.

Additional Strategies for Managing MS Fatigue

Uptime and Downtime

Many people with MS, as well as physicians who treat MS, report that engaging in an activity routine consisting of regular uptime and downtime periods is effective for combating fatigue. Alternating between more and less physically demanding or stressful activities will allow patients to increase activity levels and decrease fatigue over time.

Explain that when the patient pushes beyond what she is physically capable of, she probably experiences increased symptoms such as an increase in muscle spasms, numbness, pain or fatigue. If she pushes herself beyond what she is capable of on a daily basis, her body is always in a state of exhaustion.

If, however, she stops or changes an activity periodically when her fatigue level goes up a point or two from where it normally is, and continues to do this throughout the day, her fatigue may be no worse at the end of the day than when she began. Over time, this gives her body a chance to recuperate more effectively, because she is not regularly pushing herself to the point of exhaustion.

Emphasize that the key to this strategy is pacing. When doing various physical activities (e.g. walking, sitting, standing, vacuuming, washing dishes, or working at a computer), have the patient note how long it takes for her fatigue to go up 2 points (on the 1–10 rating scale, 1 = No fatigue—did not interfere with my ability to do things; 10 = Very fatigued—completely prevented me from doing anything). For each activity, this amount of time defines her uptime, that is, the period of time for which she should engage in that activity. For example, if a patient finds that she can fold laundry for 10 min before her baseline fatigue level of 5 goes up to 7, her uptime limit for folding laundry is 10 min.

Instruct the patient that when her uptime for any activity is over, she should change her activity to something less strenuous. A relaxation exercise, phoning a friend, reading the paper, paying bills, or doing some stretching exercises are some options. Once the patient switches to this activity, she should note how long it takes for her fatigue to go back to baseline. If it takes 15 min for her fatigue to return to baseline, her downtime requirement when she folds laundry will be 15 min.

Once the patient establishes her uptime and downtime requirements for the majority of the activities she engages in during a day, she is ready to pace herself. Whenever she engages in an activity that she knows may increase her fatigue level, she should set a timer and only do the activity for whatever uptime she has predetermined is appropriate. Then she should switch to another activity for her predesignated downtime.

When patients have used pacing for a while, they will find that they will be able to extend their uptime a little bit or decrease their downtime a bit. Explain that this is probably because the body (and mind) is not being pushed to a point of regular exhaustion. Through pacing, patients will ultimately be able to accomplish more with less frustration and fatigue. The workbook includes a Pacing Activities Worksheet to enable patients to assess their uptime and downtime periodically. You may want to help the patient fill it out in the session. Note that the Pacing Activities Worksheet is intensive. It is generally best to have specific discrete times when the patient will complete it.

Difficulties in Changing Activities or Pacing

Patients may, of course, be able to think of any number of reasons for not pacing themselves or altering their current routines:

- "I'm too busy to take a break."

- "I can't ask for help, understanding, or a change in schedule."

- "My fatigue is always the same no matter what I do."

- "If I start giving into my MS, then it is all over."

Review the strategies discussed throughout the program (e.g. using the UTD) to deal with these unhelpful thoughts about using pacing for fatigue.

Patients may have difficulty taking the lead in deciding what they can and cannot do (instead of living up to others' expectations). Stress, however, that it is absolutely essential that the patient take control. You may want to say something like the following:

> No one else can judge what you are able or not able to do. Once you have determined, through pacing, your limits and needs (as opposed to what others expect), you should notify those around you. For example, if you find that your uptime for cooking is 15 min, you can communicate this to your family and request that someone else pitch in with cooking so that more or all of the dinner cooking can be completed in about the amount of time that is your uptime.

Tell the patient that other people will generally be supportive of alterations in her routines if they are advised of the reasons and intent. They certainly will respond to her being in a better mood and feeling less fatigued.

Many people complain that while pacing themselves and setting limits on uptime at home is possible, doing so in the workplace or when caring for young children is not. It may be more difficult to use pacing strategies in these situations because of external time pressures at work in an office or at home raising kids. Inform patients that although devising pacing strategies may require more brainstorming or creative problem solving, they can be applied in the workplace and in child-rearing. For example, pacing oneself while working may require synchronizing one's efforts with the work of other people (or the uptimes and downtimes of one's children).

Once patients identify the various work tasks and their uptime and downtime requirements, encourage them to create a flow chart or diagram of how they can perform these tasks throughout the day using the pacing routine. This should include alternating between sitting tasks and standing tasks, as well as between tasks they can do individually and those that involve other people.

Common Problems in Using Pacing to Manage Fatigue

If patients find themselves needing hours or a whole day to recover during their downtime period, they have probably not stopped their uptime activity soon enough and just need to practice responding earlier to increases in fatigue or exhaustion. The Pacing Activities Worksheet will help patients fine-tune their fatigue awareness.

If patients find that delayed fatigue increases—for example, they clean out the garage one day without excessive fatigue, but the next day they feel thoroughly fatigued—then they may be experiencing the effects of deconditioning fatigue. Remember that deconditioning fatigue is a combination of decreased muscle strength and endurance that occurs as a result of not having a regular exercise routine. This is a common problem for people with MS. A regular exercise/conditioning program may be of great value in such circumstances, as it will allow patients to increase their endurance and limit muscle fatigue. Such a program may involve walking, swimming, yoga, or stretching exercises. The choice, of course, depends on the nature of the patient's symptoms and what her physical limitations are. Recommend that the patient discuss developing such a program with her neurologist or physical therapist.

Choosing What to Keep and What to Let Go

One common way to think about fatigue and energy is to consider an "Energy Bank." You may wish to say something like the following to illustrate:

> *Each day when you get up you have a certain amount of energy. This may fluctuate from day to day. Some days you may feel good, while other days may be "bad MS days." Many things you do will take energy out of the Energy Bank. But there are also things you can do that add energy. These include rest, relaxation, and, for some people, cooling off. This is not unlike uptime and downtime.*

> *But what happens when fatigue causes your overall energy level to drop? Many people continue trying to do the same amount as they did before with less energy. This is like having a reduction in income, and still trying to buy and pay for all the things you did with higher income. Eventually you will end up with a big deficit. The same thing happens with fatigue. If you keep doing and doing and doing, with less and less energy, eventually you will end up with a big deficit. Your body will tell you this by collapsing. And your spirit may collapse along with it.*

Stress that an alternative is to start making some decisions about what one wants to keep doing, what can be handed over to other people, and what one is willing to let go of.

Fatigue Goals

Because managing fatigue is so essential to the long-term management of MS, encourage the patient to write out a goal she wants to accomplish related to this module. A Fatigue Goal Worksheet is provided in the workbook. As in earlier goal-setting exercises, make sure the patient's goal is a behavioral task that can be measured in terms of the steps that she will take to accomplish it. Also assist the patient in predicting some obstacles that might make completing her goal difficult, then generating some solutions to these potential obstacles.

Review the actions to reduce fatigue and determine which might help. Encourage the patient to come up with other strategies. Often patients will come up with better solutions than those in the workbook—they know their lives and their needs better than we do. When you have finished going through the various potential changes, review the list with the patient. Come up with a reasonable set of actions for the coming week. Have the patient continue assessing her fatigue throughout the week.

Homework

✎ Have the patient monitor fatigue each day throughout the day using a Fatigue Diary.

✎ Once 5–7 days of the Fatigue Dairy are completed, have the patient start analyzing her patterns and review the section on analyzing fatigue.

✎ Have the patient complete the Pacing Activities Worksheet for activities that she does on a regular basis.

✎ Have the patient determine the main types of fatigue that impact her and a couple of strategies that she could use to better manage these types of fatigue.

✎ Assign workbook reading as appropriate.

✎ Discuss any assignments relevant to the patient's goals.

Module 3 | *Reducing Anxiety and Worry*

(Corresponds to chapter 9 of the workbook)

Materials Needed

- Copy of patient workbook
- Worry and Risk Diary
- Coping Resources Worksheet
- Estimating Probabilities Worksheet
- Thinking About the Worst-Case Scenario Worksheet
- Worry Time Worksheet
- Worry, Risk, and Resources Diary

Outline

- Set the agenda
- Rate the patient's stress/distress level
- Review homework
- Discuss anxiety and worry
- Review techniques for managing anxiety and worry
- Assign homework

Set Agenda, Obtain Stress Rating, and Review Homework

Begin the session in the usual fashion, by setting the agenda and evaluating the patient's stress or distress over the previous week. Review the homework assigned in the previous session.

Understanding Anxiety and Worry

Rates of anxiety are likely higher among people with MS than the general public. Explain that anxiety is a common response to stress and is also frequently present along with depression. Anxiety typically involves feeling anxious, nervous, on edge or restless, and excessive worrying that is difficult to control. Often anxiety is accompanied by irritability.

Anxiety involves all of the areas in the cognitive-behavioral model described in chapter 3: feelings of nervousness, anxiety, or fear; activation of the physical stress response (muscle tension, jittery stomach, more frequent sighing, sweaty palms, heart racing, etc.); thoughts (worries, "what ifs"); behavior (doing things to avoid bad things happening); and social consequences (often pushing people away either through irritability or through withdrawal). The "stress response" is described more thoroughly in module 4 on relaxation.

Worry is a key. Inform patients that if they can reduce worry, the stress response system will slow down and they will feel less anxious.

Signs of Excessive Worry

Let patients know that worry is a common response to everyday problems, but the following are signs of worrying excessively:

- It is time-consuming or constantly on your mind.

- You notice that you worry about things that others don't worry about.

- It interferes with your activities and is upsetting.

- It feels uncontrollable.

- It causes you physical problems (headaches, fatigue).

- You worry a lot without coming up with a solution.

Evaluating the Risk/Resource Ratio

Next explain that anxiety, just like other negative emotions, is often linked to unhelpful thoughts. When we face a situation that results in anxiety, we often have thoughts in two areas:

1. *Risk*: We believe the situation is threatening to us, or threatening something or someone important to us.

2. *Resources*: We have little skills or resources to deal with the situation.

These unhelpful thoughts, which make us perceive a risk, and make us believe that we do not have adequate resources to deal with the risk, can cause our anxiety system to set off a false alarm. This results in anxiety, worry, and tension.

You may want to use the following example to demonstrate how a threatening situation can change depending on our resources:

Imagine you are in the wild and you find yourself face to face with a grizzly bear—big, big paws and long claws, sharp teeth, and a nasty temper.

How scared would you be?

Now you have a big stick. How scared would you be?

Now you have a big stick and a gun. How scared would you be?

Now imagine you have a big stick, a torch, and 15 big, strong friends who all have big sticks and guns. How scared would you be?

Has the grizzly bear changed? No. Have your resources changed? Yes!!

Real Alarms vs. False Alarms

Distinguish for the patient the difference between real alarms and false alarms. You may want to say something like the following:

When dealing with a grizzly bear, anxiety and fear are a helpful response because they get you ready to fight or run away. However, in most situations in modern life, the actual danger is not as clear cut as a grizzly bear staring at you from a few feet away. In everyday situations like having problems at work, anxiety arises from situations that lack immediate danger. But unhelpful thoughts make them feel more dangerous than they are. This causes us to set off a false alarm, which includes the feelings and thoughts you would need if you were faced with a real danger. In addition, when people feel anxious and perceive danger, they often underestimate the resources they have to cope with the problem. This also leads to a false alarm.

Table M3.1 lists some examples of how people tend to overestimate risk and underestimate their resources.

Table M3.1 False alarms vs. real alarms

Risk	Resources	Alarm	Anxiety
Thinking that a problem is more likely to happen than is actually true	Not being aware of the resources that you have available	False alarm	Unhelpful anxiety
Seeing a situation as dangerous when it is actually not dangerous	Not taking into account the people (friends, family, and colleagues) who could be there to help you out	False alarm	Unhelpful anxiety
	VS.		
Real danger	Genuine lack of resources	True alarm	Helpful anxiety

This module focuses on techniques to help patients manage anxiety and worry through accurate perceptions of risk and resources. The sections that follow describe the steps to take.

Determine the Real Risk

Ask patients to recall how they identified unhelpful thoughts earlier in treatment (see chapters 6 and 7). The first step in managing anxiety is evaluating the real risk involved. If we conclude that there is no actual risk, then there is no need for a false alarm. However, if we do determine there is some degree of risk, then our goal is to determine the realistic level of risk and move to the next step: gathering resources to overcome that risk (e.g. gathering our friends and sharp sticks).

Use the Worry and Risk Worksheet in the workbook to evaluate the relationship between the patient's anxiety, worry, and risk. When the patient has identified the situation, the feeling (usually anxiety or nervousness) and the thought help him to evaluate what the true risk is. Rate the level of risk (1 = no risk, 10 = greatest risk imaginable). Here are some questions to ask the patient to help determine risk:

- "Are you making a problem out of something that's not an immediate problem?"

- "Is this situation actually risky or does it just feel that way?"

- "What is the evidence that this situation is 100% dangerous?"

- "What does this say about me and my life?"

- "What am I afraid will happen and how likely is it?"

- "What is the worst thing that could happen?"

- "What is the best thing that could happen?"

- "Am I worrying over something I have no control?"

Evaluate Coping Resources

Explain that we face situations that have some degree of risk each day, but we only have anxiety when that level of risk outweighs our ability to cope. Thus, to reduce anxiety, it is helpful to determine all of our resources available to help us cope with the threatening situation.

Use the Coping Resources Worksheet in the workbook to help the patient evaluate his resources. After the patient has completed the situation, emotions, and unhelpful thoughts, evaluate the true state of his resources. Questions to ask the patient include the following:

- "What personal and professional skills do you have to help manage this problem?"

- "What have you done to cope with problems like this in the past?"

- "What other people do you have in your life to help you deal with this?"

- "How would you cope with this if you weren't feeling anxious?"

- "How would someone else, who isn't anxious, handle the situation?"

Estimate Probability

Discuss how often, when we are excessively worried about something bad happening, we overestimate how likely it is to happen. It can be helpful to focus on figuring out the realistic chance of it actually happening and then compare it to how much your emotions tell you that it will happen. Even when you strongly feel that something bad is very likely to happen, when you start to evaluate the realistic chances, you see that the probability is actually much smaller.

Ask the patient to rate the probability that the situation he identified earlier will occur. Have the patient first estimate the probability based on his emotions and then again realistically. Usually the realistic probability is much lower than the emotional probability rating. If the realistic probability is high, it would be important to implement some problem-solving strategies. After the rating exercise, encourage the patient to come up with alternative explanations for his worry thoughts. A worksheet (Estimating Probability) is provided in the workbook.

Reduce Physical Tension

Often the physical feelings of anxiety come before the worry thoughts. Inform patients that by working every day to decrease their tension, they can decrease their overall level of anxiety. Here are some suggestions for reducing physical tension:

- Take a few deep breaths and tell yourself "relax"

- Practice relaxation exercises (see module 4 on relaxation)

- Exercise regularly

- Engage in pleasurable activities

- Take a warm bath

- Stand up and stretch during the day, especially if you work at a desk

- Get a massage or ask a loved one to rub your back

Postpone Worry and Schedule Worry Time

Sometimes people worry about not worrying. Some people think that it is important to worry because if they don't, things may fall apart. There are also some people who notice they might feel better *after* they have worried about things a little. Emphasize to patients that worrying can eat up valuable time that can be spent on more useful things.

Introduce "worry time"—a scheduled time during the day when we are allowed and even encouraged to focus on our worrying. Give patients the following instructions:

1. When worries come up during the day, write them down on a "worry list" (a Worry Time Worksheet is provided in the workbook) and avoid thinking about them for the moment.

2. Schedule some time every day to look at your list and really think about the worries you have placed on the list.

3. Limit the time to a specific amount, and stick to this time limit by planning something to do at the end of your worry time. You may want to set a kitchen timer or alarm clock whose sound will mark the end of "worry time." It is also helpful to plan something to do afterward so you don't go over your time limit (e.g. watching a favorite television show).

Let patients know that although it may feel strange at first, many people find this technique helpful. If they continue to use this technique, it will become more comfortable for them.

Worry, Risk, and Resources Diary

In the last exercise, patients put everything together in the Worry, Risk, and Resources Diary. This diary simply combines the Worry and Risk Worksheet and the Coping Resources Worksheet into one form. It focuses on the patient's unhelpful thoughts regarding the risk involved in the situation and underestimation of his resources to cope with it. The last two columns help the patient balance the true risk involved and come up with resources he has to cope with the situation. These are essentially "realistic thoughts," as were described in chapter 7 (chapter 5 of the patient workbook).

Think Through the Worst-Case Scenario

This strategy can be effective in reducing anxiety, but requires some sensitivity when applying it to people with MS. Accordingly, this strategy is not described in the workbook, but is something you can use with the patient.

This strategy identifies and focuses on the worst-case scenario. For many patients, worry is a combination of fear about an imagined outcome and avoidance of thinking about that outcome. The avoidance prevents the patient from developing strategies to manage the fears. The idea is to help the patient dig down to the worst possible fear. Sometimes as the person digs down, they realize that the fear is not so bad, and that they have the skills to manage it. In those cases, the technique is comparatively simple to use. However, MS is a disease with a great level of unpredictability, and the health and well-being consequences are potentially quite severe (although unlikely). Refer to the following example:

A woman reports being anxious because she has not performed as well as she believes she should have on a project at work. The therapist asks the patient to take a deep breath and lean back in her chair. Inducing some relaxation can help the patient manage the exercise. The therapist asks the patient to remember all aspects of the situation:

Sit back, place your arms and legs in a comfortable position, and imagine yourself in the situation you described. Try to picture all the components of the situation. For example, imagine the people, sights, sounds, colors, smells, etc . . . As you mentally put yourself in that difficult situation, try to focus on aspects of the situation that are likely to be problematic or troubling for you.

Once the patient has described the situation, the therapist asks what the patient is afraid of (see the following dialogue).

Patient: I am afraid that my supervisor will get upset with me.

Therapist: And if your supervisor got upset with you, then what would happen?

Patient: I don't know, she might yell. I might get fired.

Therapist: And if you got fired, then what?

Patient: Well, then I wouldn't have any income. I'd lose my health insurance. And I might not be able to find a job.

Therapist: So if all those things happened—no income, no health insurance, no job—what are you worried might happen then?

Patient: I couldn't pay rent—I'd end up on the street. I'd have no treatment for my MS—that would get worse. I could end up having exacerbations, becoming completely disabled and living on the street . . .

At this point there are several potential directions the therapist can take. The first is to use the risk and resource evaluation technique described earlier. Ask the patient to evaluate the probability of this happening. The emotional probability is likely higher than the realistic probability. Nevertheless, for many MS patients, such fears of deterioration are quite vivid. Ask the patient how he might cope with each step so that he can assemble his resources. It is helpful to write these down for the patient. Then ask the patient if he has noticed any changes in his feelings of anxiety, now that he has reviewed these options.

It may also be useful to point out how far the patient is extrapolating from a simple situation. For example:

> *So you start out being concerned about the quality of one piece of your work, and then very quickly you are imagining yourself homeless and disabled on the street.*

Some patients will see absurdity in this, which can be useful.

Helping the patient manage arousal through relaxation (see module 4) will also provide the patient with the tools to control the physical aspects of the anxiety.

If the patient responds well to this intervention in session, you can assign it as a homework assignment. However, it is best to evaluate the patient's response in session before suggesting that the patient perform it by himself.

Homework

- Have the patient complete the Worry, Risk, and Resources Diary at least once a day for the next week.

- Encourage the patient to practice each of the anxiety and worry management strategies at least once in the next week.

- Assign workbook reading as appropriate. If the patient has high levels of anxiety, module 4 on relaxation may be useful.

- Discuss any assignments relevant to the patient's goals.

Module 4 *Relaxation*

(Corresponds to chapter 10 of the workbook)

Materials Needed

- Copy of patient workbook
- Guided imagery script

Outline

- Set the agenda
- Rate the patient's stress/distress level
- Review homework
- Describe the physical stress response system
- Review relaxation techniques for controlling stress
- Teach deep breathing
- Emphasize the importance of relaxation practice
- Assign homework

Therapist Note

■ *Core chapters (3–8) of this program taught patients how to manage stress by changing what they do and how they think. This module focuses on how to gain control over the physical stress response system.* ■

Set Agenda, Obtain Stress Rating, and Review Homework

Begin the session in the usual fashion, by setting the agenda and evaluating the patient's stress or distress over the previous week. Review the homework assigned in the previous session.

How the Body Creates and Reduces the Experience of Stress

Before describing how to control the stress response, use the following information to explain what is happening biologically when someone experiences a stressful event. Our nervous system has two subsystems—the sympathetic nervous system and the parasympathetic nervous system. These two systems are controlled like an internal thermostat. The sympathetic nervous system is equivalent to a heating system. When we experience something stressful, we become aroused and stress hormones (such as cortisol) are produced. These stress hormones increase bodily activities like heart rate, breathing, muscle tension, blood pressure, and perspiration. This system of arousal was designed to prepare the body for fight or flight (e.g. when confronted by a lion).

While the sympathetic nervous system heats up the body, the parasympathetic nervous system acts as a cooling system. The parasympathetic nervous system brings the body's reactions back to normal by producing a relaxation response that slows down the heart rate and breathing, relaxes the muscles, and lowers blood pressure.

The stress thermostat function runs smoothly by gauging the heating and cooling precisely, heating up a bit when we perceive a stressful situation, cooling down when the situation has passed. This system works well when there is an occasional stressor. However, when someone experiences ongoing stress, or if the body is constantly responding to stress, the thermostat heats up, cools down, heats up, and cools down—over and over—and eventually the thermostat breaks down. The heating system stays on but the cooling system does not get activated. When the thermostat breaks, it requires a manual setting of the cooling system.

Inform patients that relaxation can be like the manual setting of the cooling system. Relaxation exercises reduce feelings of stress by slowing heart rate, slowing breathing, lowering blood pressure, and relaxing muscles. Relaxation practice can be used in two ways:

- If the patient is under chronic stress, relaxation practice can help her get control over her stress thermostat, and get her nervous system and stress response system back in sync. This will help the patient feel overall more calm and in control.

- If the patient practices relaxation regularly, she will also develop better control over her physical stress response system (heart rate, muscle tension, blood pressure, breathing, etc.). This will allow the patient much greater control over her body's ability to quickly cool down her stress response system when stressful events occur.

The Basics of Relaxation

The core principle of relaxation is breathing. Explain that deep breathing is one of the easiest, most effective ways to reduce tension in the body. Learning to be aware of and to control one's breathing is the first step toward controlling the physical and mental effects of stress. There are two types of breathing: chest and abdominal.

Chest Breathing

Inform the patient that most people are chest breathers. Chest breathing is shallow. The shoulders often rise with each breath and only the chest expands. This results in poor exchange of stale air for fresh air. This also contributes to fatigue, because the body's cells aren't able to receive the oxygen necessary for effective functioning. People tend to increase shallow chest breathing when stressed. Conversely, shallow breathing can contribute to feelings of stress.

Abdominal Breathing

Abdominal breathing involves slow, deep breaths using the diaphragm. The diaphragm is a large sheet of muscle, like a piece of a rubber balloon, stretched over the bottom of the lungs. When breathing is relaxed, the diaphragm expands down on the in-breath, creating a negative pressure that pulls air into the lungs. On the out-breath, the diaphragm relaxes back into its original position, pushing air out of the lungs. When the diaphragm moves down on the in-breath, the contents of the abdomen are naturally moved forward so that the abdomen expands. If we place our hands on our abdomen, we will feel it bulge out on the in-breath and flatten back on the out-breath.

Emphasize to the patient that learning to breathe with the diaphragm will help the body automatically shift from the stress mode to the relaxed mode. If the patient continues slow, deep abdominal breathing for several minutes, her heartbeat will slow, blood pressure will drop, blood circulation will increase—basically the nervous system will reset to a "cooled down" state—a state of physical relaxation rather than stress. As she becomes physically more relaxed, she should also begin to feel emotionally more relaxed. Once these basics are described, invite the patient to try a 3-min deep breathing exercise.

Deep Breathing Exercise

Ask the patient to rate her tension from 0 to 10, with 10 being the most tense she's ever been. Then give the following instructions using a calm, measured voice:

> *Take a moment to make yourself comfortable—loosen any tight clothing, stretch for a second to remove any obvious points of tension.*
>
> *Sit comfortably in a chair or lie down.*

If the patient is in a chair, be sure her back is straight, her shoulders are back, and her feet are flat on the floor. Some people find it helpful to imagine a thread attached to the top of their head, pulling their head up to the heavens, elongating their neck and spine. Ask the patient to sit comfortably, with a sense of dignity.

> *Close your eyes, and focus your attention on your breath. Breathe mainly through your nose. You can leave your mouth closed, or slightly open—whichever allows the muscles in the jaw to feel most relaxed. Breathe slowly into your abdomen. When you've completed inhaling,*

hold your breath for a few seconds before exhaling. This helps slow your breathing. Feel your belly rising and falling. If this is the first time you are doing this, you may want to place your hand on your belly to feel it rising and falling.

Bring your attention to your breathing. Notice the feeling of your belly expanding and contracting. Maybe you feel your clothes against your belly. Or you sense the feeling of cool air entering your nose on the inhale, and warm air exiting on your exhale. [Wait quietly for 10–15 s.]

Notice any places you have muscle tension. As you exhale, see if you can let go of just a bit of that tension. You might imagine the tension flowing out on your exhaled breath. [Wait quietly for 15–30 s.]

When any noises occur, incorporate them into the exercise—for example:

If you hear noises around you, just notice them. You don't need to be bothered. There is nothing you need to do about them. If you want, you can label them, like "Ah, a car honking" or "A dog barking" [use whatever noises are actually occurring].

Continue the exercise for a total of 3–5 min. Then ask the patient to rerate her tension level. If it has dropped, ask her what she makes of that, and underscore the effectiveness of this exercise. If it did not drop significantly, let her know that with practice, she will gain more control over her tension and be able to reduce it using breathing and relaxation exercises.

This breathing technique is a core to almost all relaxation exercises. Let the patient know that she can use this exercise anytime she is feeling stressed or tense. It is a good tool to reset the nervous system. Also let her know that if she practices on a regular basis, she will get better at this, and will learn to reduce tension very rapidly, sometimes even with a couple of breaths.

Therapist Note

■ *A small number of people sometimes have a "paradoxical response" to some forms of relaxation. They find that they become panicky when engaging in relaxation (they find their breath speeds up, their heart starts racing, they become quite anxious and fearful). If this happens, discontinue relaxation. Assess the phenomenon to see if there is any history of such panic. Are the conditions in which the patient is able to relax? If so, try to incorporate those features into the practice.*

Such reactions may be associated with a need to not lose control. Some people may be more comfortable with their eyes open. You might suggest the patient direct her gaze at a blank or nonmoving surface like the floor or wall, and then allow herself to slightly unfocus. You might also try having the patient give herself the instructions either mentally or out loud in a soft voice. ∎

Types of Relaxation

There are many different types of relaxation. A few are described in the patient's workbook.

Progressive Muscle Relaxation (PMR). This exercise is often used to teach people who have either never tried relaxation before or not done it in some time. The basic idea is simply to tense muscle groups, and then let go. Using diaphragmatic breathing and letting go after tensing helps to relax the muscles. This is an excellent place for some people to start. However, this exercise may not be appropriate for people with spasticity, because the tensing may aggravate pain.

Deep Breathing. The focus of this exercise is on increasing awareness of breath and using breath to control arousal. This is a core part of any relaxation exercise, and is essentially the exercise described previously.

Guided Imagery. This exercise uses mental imagery to help achieve a sense of calm. Typically a recording helps the patient create images that can help her enter a relaxed state. Many people find this a very easy and enjoyable way of relaxing. However, some people find the voices and sounds distracting.

Meditation. Many meditation exercises involve observing your experiences, such as your breath, sounds, or thoughts. Joining a meditation group is highly recommended to increase the likelihood that the patient will continue.

Mindfulness. Mindfulness is a specific form of meditation that has become very popular in recent years.

Yoga and Tai Chi. These are exercises that involve some movement, but are intended to increase relaxation.

Encourage the patient to try as many different types of relaxation as possible. Some people like relaxation exercises that involve audiotapes or CDs. Others prefer quiet exercises. Some people like exercises in which there is no movement while other people like the movement that Yoga and Tai Chi use. Emphasize to the patient that there is no "right exercise" or "right way" to perform it.

Learning to Relax

It is important to conduct relaxation exercises in the office with the patient so that you can teach her how to do them, answer questions, address problems, observe the patient for any signs of difficulties, and check how well they work for the patient.

Therapist Note

■ *There are a few nuances to conducting relaxation exercises with MS patients. First, if the patient has spasticity, do not use exercises that require tensing the muscle groups where the spasticity is present. This can induce cramping or cause pain. Also, you may have your own methods of inducing relaxation. Avoid using imagery that may be related to MS symptoms or problems. For example, many relaxation induction techniques suggest sensory changes such as feeling limbs as being heavy, numb, or tingly. These are all MS symptoms, and so may trigger anxiety and arousal rather than relaxation. It is best to simply avoid the use of sensory suggestions unless you are certain that the patient does not have those symptoms. Likewise, many relaxation inductions use suggestions of warmth, or imagery such as imagining taking a warm bath. For patients with heat sensitivity, such suggestions may also have negative associations. We have used "imagining yourself floating in a comfortably cool stream" for patients with heat sensitivity. The suggestion has the effect of shifting consciousness, just as the sensory suggestions are intended, and therefore can contribute to a relaxed state.* ■

Relaxation Exercises

As a therapist you likely have many relaxation exercises at your disposal, and we encourage you to use anything you are comfortable with and that you feel the patient will respond to. PMR and the body scan are two relaxation exercises described in the patient workbook. Both of these are good places to start for people who have not had much experience with relaxation (again, avoid or adapt the PMR exercise as necessary for patients with spasticity). In the following section, a guided imagery relaxation exercise that suggests immune system enhancement has been provided. It is important to note that this exercise is not intended to have an effect on the immune system above and beyond what any relaxation exercise has. You might introduce it by saying something like the following:

> *If you practice relaxation on a regular basis, it may have a positive effect on your overall health and on your immune system. This is a guided imagery exercise that uses imagery from the immune system. Now this exercise is not necessarily any better for you than any other, but I've found many patients like it. Would you like to try it?*

Immune-Focused Relaxation Strategy

Before you begin, ask the patient to rate her tension on a scale from 0 to 10.

> *Go ahead and find a comfortable position, sitting either in a chair or on the floor. If you feel more comfortable lying down, you may do that instead. Now, if you are comfortable, I would like you to close your eyes, or just gaze softly down at the floor. And, I would like you to turn your attention to your breathing . . . breathing into your belly, and out* [note—it is helpful to time the "in" and "out" to the patient's inhale and exhale] . . . *Notice the regular rate, rhythm, and volume of your breaths . . . Notice how with each breath in, your stomach gently rises . . . and with each breath out, your stomach slowly falls . . . I would like you to prepare for your first deep, belly breath, inhaling through your nose . . . and holding for your count of 3 . . . 2 . . . 1 . . . And release the air through your mouth, feeling the*

warm air whooshing out. Now allow your regular pattern of breathing to resume . . . [pause for 15 s]. Again, inhale through your nose, drawing more air into your belly, completely filling your lungs with air . . . and hold for your count of 3 . . . 2 . . . 1 . . . and then slowly, slowly release the air through your mouth . . . noticing the warm air and feeling of relaxation spreading . . . And, again, allow your breathing to return to a regular rhythm, and feel yourself breathing in a pattern that is comfortable for you. [Pause for 15 s . . .]

As I speak, you can pay attention to words, or not, as you choose. The only thing that is important right now is how you feel . . . calm . . . peaceful . . . relaxed . . . If you want, you can begin—with each breath—to notice tension melting away and you may begin to feel your body becoming lighter . . . as though you are carrying less and less weight. And, as you become lighter, you sense a light . . . you can see it coming . . . maybe it starts as a small pin-sized light . . . maybe you can see it coming from inside of you . . . Either way, allow the light to grow and envelop you in a soothing, calming embrace . . . As the light surrounds you, you feel it, soothing and gentle . . . it carries you . . . floating . . . soothing . . . calming . . . supporting . . . healing. The light carries you through space . . . and you find yourself floating, and surrounded by this soft, healing light. You feel safe, cared for. Connected. [Pause for 20 s . . .]

Breathe in the light, feel the light inside you . . . moving gently into your lungs . . . and through your lungs . . . into your blood stream . . . and into your heart . . . feel the light throughout your belly and chest, glowing brighter with each breath in . . . feel the light move in to your back, into your spine . . . feel your chest and spine fill with the bright, healing light . . . as the nerves in your spine fill with healing light, bringing a gentle strength . . . Feel how it is both powerful and calming at the same time . . . feel the light grow out from the nerves into the spine, relieving tension in each vertebrae . . . Perhaps you can feel this bright, calming, healing light moving out through your nerves to other parts of the body . . . down into the lower back . . . down into the thighs . . . the calves . . . all way down into the feet. Feel with each breath how the light comes in to your belly and chest, and flows down into the lower back, thighs, calves, and feet . . . each breath bringing a calming, healing light . . . Perhaps you also feel that the healing light moves out from your chest into the shoulders, through the nerves and blood vessels, into your shoulders and upper arms . . . into your forearms . . . hands . . . and fingers . . . Let the gentle, calming, healing light flow throughout your body with each breath . . . feel the light moving up through your neck . . . feel the light envelop your head and brain . . . an embracing, healing light . . . Allow the light to course throughout your body, healing, calming, embracing . . . Perhaps you can feel your body's life energy . . . feel it strengthening . . . [Pause for 20–30 s . . .]

If there is a part of your body that worries you, from MS or for any other reason, bring it to mind . . . If many parts come to mind, allow one to come forward. Know that you can choose another part next time. Don't worry about choosing the right part to focus on . . . Just allow the healing light to flow into the part of the body . . . and allow the light to bring a gentle enveloping calm . . . allow your body to accept this healing and soothing light. Allow it to calm the immune system . . . as you feel the light moving through, see it: glowing . . . calming . . . healing . . . Allow the light to surround your nerves . . . calming . . . healing . . . relaxing . . . [Pause for 15–20 s . . .]

Notice that each time you inhale, you inhale the light that surrounds you . . . the light becomes brighter . . . even more calming . . . As you exhale, you exhale the darkness of whatever bad feelings you have . . . the fatigue, or pain, or tightness, or whatever you feel . . . you can see it flowing out of you on each breath that you exhale . . . Feel the light move through your body . . . through the nervous system . . . coursing through . . . And each time you inhale, the gentle power becomes stronger . . . calming the nerves . . . healing the nerves . . . Each time you exhale, you release more of the bad feelings or physical pains . . . these just flow out of you . . . Allow that light to stay with you . . . bright . . . calming . . . soothing . . . healing . . . [Pause for 1–2 min . . .]

Continue to breathe gently . . . noticing perhaps that your regular rate, rhythm, and volume of air has changed. You may notice deeper, slower breaths. And feel the oxygen carried through your veins . . . Keeping your eyes closed, gently begin to notice the world outside of you . . . Notice the sounds . . . perhaps of your breathing, or of others . . . Notice the textures . . . Of your clothes on your skin . . . of the support from the chair, floor, or wall . . . You can let the light stay inside you, or if you prefer, allow it to slowly fade, leaving its calmness, soothing and relaxing, behind. As you bring yourself back, remember this calmness . . . this kindness . . . gentleness . . . and know that you can return to this at any time you choose.

Continue breathing, keeping your eyes closed as long as you like. When you are ready, open your eyes, and come back to the room, feeling calmer, soothed, and at peace.

Finding Support for Relaxation

It is helpful if patients can find support outside of therapy to continue their relaxation. Most communities offer a variety of meditation and yoga classes. Many local MS society chapters have also begun offering Yoga and Tai Chi tailored specifically for people with MS. Classes can be very useful in helping people practice on a regular basis. It is also nice way for people to meet other people who have similar interests. Encourage your patient to look into these resources.

Many patients also find it helpful to have audio recordings of relaxation exercises. There are many relaxation exercises available for free on the Internet. These are audio or video files that can be played directly from the site, or downloaded for use at any time. Search under "relaxation exercise" or "relaxation exercise and audio"; several sites should be readily available. At the time of this writing, several universities have provided a variety of relaxation exercises on their Web sites, including the University of Wisconsin at http://forms.uhs.wisc.edu/relaxation.php, the University of Pittsburgh Medical Center at http://healthylifestyle.upmc.com/StressRelaxation. htm, and Loyola University at www.loyola.edu/campuslife/ healthservices/counselingcenter/relaxation.html. These exercises are of all different lengths, from a few minutes to 15 min. Some include basic instruction while others do not. Some have just a voice, while some include music or other sounds. Encourage your patient to try different exercises.

Emphasize that practicing relaxation is one of the most critical aspects of stress management training. *Study after study has shown that practicing relaxation has profound benefits on stress hormones, the immune system, and, perhaps most importantly, a person's sense of well-being.* The more the patient practices, the better she will become at controlling her body's response to stressful events.

It is best to practice at a set time once a day. However, if the patient does not feel she can practice each day, select a target number of times she thinks she can practice in the coming week. While once a day is optimal, it is better to set a realistic and achievable goal, than to have one that the patient knows she cannot make.

Review the following tips for relaxation practice:

■ Practice in a quiet part of your home where you are not likely to be disturbed.

■ Do not practice after taking stimulants such as coffee or cigarettes.

■ Avoid practicing after using alcohol or drugs that change your thinking.

■ If you have trouble sleeping, try doing relaxation right before going to bed.

■ If you have stressful days, try doing relaxation in the morning.

Having patients keep track of their relaxation, as well as how effective it is in reducing tension, will help them track their progress in learning how to control their tension and arousal. Most people find at the beginning that their tension does not go down much after practice. But after a few weeks of consistent practice, patients will likely notice that relaxation substantially reduces tension. Have patients use the Relaxation Log in the workbook to keep track of the kinds of relaxation exercises they use, and to rate their level of tension before and after the exercise on a scale from 1 (no tension) to 10 (extreme tension).

Homework

✏ Have the patient practice relaxation. Help the patient choose a time of day, frequency of practice, and length of practice that works best for her.

✏ Check if the patient wants to search for relaxation recordings on the Internet, or if she would like to find a mediation, yoga, or Tai Chi group.

✏ Have the patient keep track of relaxation practice on the Relaxation Log in the workbook and notice tension before and after each exercise.

✏ After the patient has been practicing for a week, and feels that she is able to control her level of stress and arousal at least somewhat, have her begin trying the 3-min deep breathing exercise at least once a day when she experiences tension.

✏ Assign workbook reading as appropriate.

✏ Discuss any assignments relevant to the patient's goals.

Module 5 | *Pain Management*

(Corresponds to chapter 11 of the workbook)

Materials Needed

- Copy of patient workbook
- Pain Diary
- Challenging Unhelpful Thoughts Diary
- 3 × 5 cards
- Reframing Worksheet

Outline

- Set the agenda
- Rate the patient's stress/distress level
- Review homework
- Discuss sources of pain
- Discuss types of pain
- Discuss treatment of pain
- Introduce self-monitoring using a pain diary
- Discuss relaxation and pain
- Present strategies in the coping toolbox for pain
- Assign homework

Set Agenda, Obtain Stress Rating, and Review Homework

Begin the session in the usual fashion, by setting the agenda and evaluating the patient's stress or distress over the previous week. Review the homework assigned in the previous session.

Sources of Pain

Pain, like fatigue or numbness, is a symptom that many people with MS experience. Estimates indicate that up to two-thirds of MS patients experience pain. Review the various aspects of pain:

Biologically: pain is a signal that body tissue has been harmed, including the central nervous system.

Psychologically: pain is experienced as emotional suffering.

Behaviorally: pain alters the way a person moves and acts.

Cognitively: pain is associated with thoughts and attributions about its meaning, cause, consequences, and possible remedies.

Explain while the biological origin of most pain is from tissue damage, psychological, behavioral, and cognitive factors can play a substantial role in how pain is experienced. This module covers coping strategies aimed at several of these components of pain.

Types of MS Pain

There are several types of MS pain. Having pain does not necessarily indicate greater severity of MS. Some are acute while others are chronic. Understanding the types of pain will help the patient access adequate medical care.

Acute Pain

Trigeminal neuralgia. The trigeminal nerve goes into the cheek, jaw, and back of the eye. This type of pain can have sharp, shooting spasms or a continuous burning type of dull ache. Facial movement makes this type of pain worse. This type of pain can sometimes feel like dental pain. These are often treated with anticonvulsant drugs like carbamazepine (Tegretol®) or phenytoin (Dilantin®).

Dysesthesias. These types of pain are experienced as burning or aching in the extremities or in your body. When it is in the body it is also called "girdling" or the "MS Hug." This type of pain is often treated with the anticonvulsant gabapentin (Neurontin®) or with antidepressants such as amitryptline (Elavin®), duloxetine hydrocholoride (Cymblata®), or pregabalin (Lyrica®). Over-the-counter acetaminophen can also be helpful.

There are a couple of other useful remedies for dysesthesias. Many people find wearing a pressure stocking or glove helps by converting the pain sensations to sensations of pressure. Warm compresses can convert feelings of pain to feelings of warmth.

Lhermitte's sign. This is a brief, stabbing, or electric shock sensation that runs from the back of the head down the spine. It is brought on by bending the neck forward. Useful medications include the anticonvulsants mentioned above. In addition, a soft collar to limit neck movement can be useful.

Chronic Pain

Dysesthesias. Some of the pain mentioned above, particularly feelings of burning, aching, and "pins and needles," can also be chronic. The treatments are the same as described under acute dysesthesias above.

Spasticity. Pain from spasticity can come from spasms of cramps. Medications for the spasticity include baclofen (Lioresal®) or tizanidine (Zanaflex®). Pain is usually managed with anti-inflammatory medications such as ibuprofen. In addition, exercises such as stretching are important. Spasticity can also be reduced by balancing water intake with adequate sodium and potassium, because shortages of these minerals can cause muscle cramps.

Pain in the back and muscles. Secondary pain that develops in the back and muscles may be because of several causes. For example, when a person repeatedly alters how he walks (say, because of primary leg pain or because of spasticity), back pain may develop over time because of poor mechanics. Or, if a person reduces his level of activity because of fatigue, muscle strength may deteriorate and eventually lead to back pain or pain in another area. Similarly, secondary back pain may result from postural problems. Sitting or standing too long can aggravate back pain—this can be particularly difficult for people who use wheelchairs, scooters, or who otherwise spend long periods of time sitting.

Tension headaches are another type of secondary pain that is common in MS. Headaches may develop because of the stresses of living with a chronic disease. In addition, headaches can be caused by chronic muscle tension in other parts of the body, such as the neck, jaw, shoulders, or upper back.

Treatments for this type of pain include correcting the problems with walking and posture. This may involve strengthening exercises, massage, ultrasound, or the use of aids. A physical therapist can assist with this. Heat on the affected areas can also sometimes reduce pain.

While there are many pharmacological and medical treatments that can be effective, most people find that some residual pain remains. As we describe at the beginning of this chapter, pain can have a considerable impact on our emotions, thoughts, and behaviors. Pain is known to cause increases in depression and anxiety. It causes worry and rumination. And pain can cause us to reduce our activities. All of this together can result in significant reductions in our quality of life. The remaining portion of this chapter describes pain management strategies that can be the focus of the stress and mood management program.

Self-Monitoring Using a Pain Diary

Explain that one important way to gain control over pain is for the patient to record it so that he can see how certain factors—time of day, overactivity or underactivity, the weather, tension, and sleeplessness—increase or decrease his pain levels. Recording helps to identify the location, type, quality, severity, and duration of pain, as well as things that reduce or increase pain.

Stress that monitoring should be done three times a day, at regular times that are convenient for the patient. For example, he might record his pain level when he awakens, after lunch, and then again at bedtime. Explain to the patient that recording pain on a schedule rather than only when he experiences pain is important so that he learns about when his pain worsens and also when it decreases. In other words, recording the pain at regular intervals will allow the patient to detect, over time, whether there are any patterns to his pain. These patterns will allow the patient to identify the factors that increase or decrease his pain. The patient can then gain more control over his pain by increasing activities or factors that reduce pain and decreasing activities that worsen pain.

Some people are resistant to the idea of monitoring their pain, and the patient may be one of those people. It is hard enough to be in pain, and it is an additional hassle to have to think about and record it three times a day. The patient may think that focusing on his pain so much will only make it worse. You can tell him that surprisingly, keeping a pain diary is not typically associated with increased pain reports. Rather, people who keep pain diaries often report that doing so helps them feel better. You may want to encourage the patient by saying something like the following:

> If you don't think recording your pain will be a chore, that's great. If you do, consider this: You have done your best in your current situation, and yet you are not satisfied with how your pain is being managed. Recording your pain levels can help you determine where you might be stuck and point you in the direction of better pain management. You can't count on remembering exactly what your pain feels like under all conditions over a long period of time. So give the recording method a shot—it might just work for you.

Explain that the pain diary can also be an important source of information when he sees his healthcare provider, particularly when the two of them are tracking the patient's treatment responses or symptom flare-ups.

Keeping a Pain Diary

To illustrate, complete a pain diary with the patient that is representative of his day up until the appointment with you. It may be useful to review the sample pain diary for the case example of Judy provided in chapter 11 of the workbook first (Figure 11.1).

Explain that it is important to differentiate between *pain sensation* and *pain distress* on the pain diary. *Pain sensation* refers to the physical component of pain—the achiness, stabbing, burning, tightness, and other physical sensations the patient has. *Pain distress* refers to how the patient feels about the pain or how much the pain bothers him at that moment (e.g. frustrated, angry, anxious, or sad).

Emphasize that the pain diary is intended for the patient's benefit and self-exploration. Therefore, if he finds it more helpful to record pain in two separate areas of the body or would like to differentiate pain distress from more general life distress, encourage him to do so. A blank Pain Diary for the patient's use is provided in chapter 11 (module 5) of the workbook. It is a good idea to begin filling out a Pain Diary together in session.

Relaxation and Pain

If the patient has been keeping a Pain Diary, he may have recognized by now that pain is often associated with some form of increased muscle tension. This muscle tension can either precede or follow pain sensation, and may feel like an automatic reaction to the pain. The patient may have noticed that he tends to experience muscle tension in a specific location (e.g. clenching of the hands, tightening of the jaw, teeth grinding, shallow breathing or holding of the breath, overall soreness in muscles, etc).

If the patient has not done so, he should read chapter 10 on relaxation (module 4) in the workbook. Inform the patient that research has shown that regular, daily practice of relaxation exercises can reduce muscle tension and the severity of pain episodes. The patient's awareness of when he tends to experience muscle tension can help him identify times in which it may be beneficial to practice a relaxation strategy in order to release the muscle tension. Simply breathing deeply for a minute can help reduce tension in the moment.

In addition to reducing muscle tension, the patient can use relaxation tools to cope with immediate pain symptoms by changing his focus from the pain to his breathing, to external sounds, or whatever method of relaxation he prefers. You may want to say something like the following:

> *You may have noticed that on days when your pain is bad, your attention becomes focused on the pain and you have trouble concentrating. You may also lose your appetite, or even become a bit nauseous. Conversely, you may have found that when you are intensely focused on an activity (such as watching an engaging movie or talking with your best friend), your perception of pain impulses, for that time, slips out of awareness. Relaxation methods, in addition to reducing tension, can similarly be used to manage pain by shifting focus off the pain.*

For some people, *mindfulness*, a strategy related to relaxation, can be helpful. With this strategy, patients manage pain by intently focusing on one specific location of the pain and imagining breathing into it. Explain that by being mindful of the pain we are attempting to maintain a meditative focus on one area. This type of mind focus seems to reduce overall tension and pain. Audio recordings of mindfulness exercises are available for free on many Internet sites, by searching "mindfulness exercise" or "mindfulness exercise and audio." At the time of this writing, one site offering a mindfulness exercise is at the University of Vermont is www.uvm.edu/~chwb/counseling/mindfulness/mindfulnessaudio.html.

Coping Tool Box for Pain

Review the following additional strategies for coping with pain. As one method does not work for everyone, encourage the patient to try several methods to see which are most effective for him.

Coping Card

After the patient has experimented with and become familiar with various ways of managing pain, encourage him to create a *coping card*. On a 3 × 5 card, have the patient list several different things that he can do to manage his pain. Suggest to the patient that he carry this *coping card* in his wallet, and refer to it whenever he needs help coping with pain. Just having the *coping card* with them can help patients feel better because they will feel more confident in their ability to cope with their pain.

Reframing Unhelpful Thoughts

Another tool for managing pain involves an examination of the relationship between thoughts or feelings and pain. Explain that this approach is based on the premise that many moods, emotions, and feelings are sustained, if not created, by self-talk. If we alter or reframe the way we talk to ourselves about pain, we can actually change our pain experience. Self-talk is automatic, happens very quickly, and isn't always phrased in complete sentences. See if the patient can provide you examples from his experience. If you need an example, you can use the following from the workbook:

> For example, imagine that you wake up in the morning and open your eyes. When you attempt to get out of bed, you become aware of pain in your body, and you think to yourself, "It's still here. Ugh! I can't stand it anymore! When will it go away? I've suffered enough. I'm useless! I'll never get better. This is going to be a miserable day. Life is miserable. I'm miserable. No one cares." If you talk to yourself like this, why wouldn't you feel sad or very upset?

You can also tell patients that research shows that when people feel depressed or their mood is poor, they report more pain.

Explain that there is another reason why this kind of self-talk can make one feel worse. Many of these thoughts have to do with the pain being out of control, unbearable, and never-ending. When we feel like we have no control over unpleasant things (such as pain), and see no end to the unpleasantness, we experience the situation as more aversive than if we feel like we can control the unpleasantness or that it will be short-lived. Thus, when we tell ourselves, "I can't take this," "this is unbearable," or "this will never stop," we may feel worse. If we can replace those thoughts with ones that are more realistic, adaptive, and convey more control (such as "I don't like this, but I can handle it"), we may feel better.

Emphasize that the patient has the ability to change his self-talk. He can begin reframing his thoughts by using one of the two techniques described below. Demonstrate the first technique, using a Challenging Unhelpful Thoughts Diary for his pain. Ideally you will be able to have the patient complete the diary from a recent session. However, if you need an example, you can use the case study of Judy in chapter 11 of the workbook (Figure 11.3). Review how, by substituting more realistic thoughts for negative automatic thoughts, the patient will be able to reduce the intensity of his negative emotions.

Clarifying the Problem and What Can Be Done

A second reframing exercise can help patients to clarify the real problem after the negative self-talk has been identified. It also serves to give them an idea of where they have the control or power in a seemingly impossible situation. Using Judy's problem as an example, review the following steps:

1. State the problem.
    Example: *I am awakening in pain.*

2. State why it's a problem.
    Example: *Because I had plans to visit a friend today.*

3. Identify: What can you do?
    Example: *I will see how I feel after taking a hot shower, practicing a relaxation technique, and taking two aspirin.*

4. What do you need?
    Example: *I can ask that my friend come here, or that we meet somewhere closer to my house. Or I can visit another time. This happens. It is usually time-limited. I know what I can do to take care of myself.*

5. How do you feel?
   Example: *Disappointed, but in control.*

Have the patient pick a problem and help him work through the steps of reframing. A blank Reframing Worksheet is provided in the workbook.

Common patient responses to using the coping techniques that have been outlined in this chapter are: *This can't possibly make a difference— my pain is real. I'm in too much pain to focus on this. What will people think if they see me doing nothing? I do so little as it is. My family needs me.* Let patients know that the coping and reframing techniques discussed in this chapter will not make everything that happens to them stress- or pain-free. However, they can allow patients to identify their choices and control their responses to life's daily hassles and major challenges rather than being controlled by pain.

Homework

✎ Have the patient monitor pain using a Pain Diary. Help the patient pick three times a day to fill out the schedule (e.g. morning, noon, and before going to bed). Also encourage the patient to complete a Pain Diary entry whenever he actually has pain.

✎ Have the patient complete at least three Challenging Unhelpful Thoughts Diaries to better manage his reactions to pain and reduce the intensity of pain.

✎ Have the patient try using the coping and problem-solving technique, completing the Reframing Worksheet as needed.

✎ If the patient has not done so, instruct him to read chapter 10 (module 4) on relaxation in the workbook.

✎ If the patient has completed the relaxation module, he should continue to practice relaxation exercises. Consider suggesting a mindfulness strategy (many audio mindfulness exercises are available on the Internet).

Therapist Note

■ *Those relaxation exercises that focus on breathing, thoughts, and sounds are more likely to be helpful to more people. Some people find focusing on sensations helpful, but some people find that can increase awareness of pain.* ■

■ Assign workbook reading as appropriate.

■ Discuss any assignments relevant to the patient's goals.

Module 6 | *Planning and Organization*

(Corresponds to chapter 12 of the workbook)

Materials Needed

- Copy of patient workbook
- To-do list form
- Planning My Day form
- My Overwhelming Tasks form

Outline

- Set the agenda
- Review the patient's stress/distress level
- Review homework
- Discuss the importance of planning and organization
- Introduce using an organizer
- Introduce making to-do lists
- Help the patient set realistic goals
- Address obstacles that interfere with planning and organization
- Assign homework

Begin the session in the usual fashion, by setting the agenda and evaluating the patient's stress or distress over the previous week. Review the homework assigned in the previous session.

Why Look at Planning and Organization?

Planning and organization is a central part of coping with MS. For many people, the stress of modern life has made planning and organization an essential part of everyday life. Improving planning and organizational abilities is also a way to deal with common cognitive symptoms such as difficulties with memory, concentration, or thinking.

The patient workbook provides an overview of the types of cognitive problems commonly experienced by people with MS, including cognitive slowing, problems with attention and concentration, and problems with memory, among others. Also, review the discussion of cognitive impairment in MS in chapter 1 of this guide.

There are a few treatments available for cognitive problems. Some of the disease-modifying medications such as interferons have been shown to slow the development of cognitive impairments. There are also some medications to treat cognitive symptoms. A few studies have shown improvements in attention with computerized cognitive training programs, although this sort of rehabilitation is still experimental. For most people, the benefits of these drugs and rehabilitation programs are at best modest, but may nevertheless be worth considering. If patients would like more information on such medication or cognitive rehabilitation programs, urge them to discuss this with their doctors. The most commonly used tool for managing cognitive impairment remains developing good planning and organizational skills. You may want to say something like the following to the patient:

> *You may not have much control over the state of your memory and thinking. However, if you think of memory and thinking problems as ones that involve planning and organization, this will give you leverage and control over how these symptoms impact your life. You do*

have some control over the degree to which you can plan and organize your life. The more you can substitute good organizational skills for memory problems, the better you will be able to function.

Regardless of the patient's level of MS symptoms, she will probably find some benefit from improved planning and organizational skills. Ask if the patient finds that she periodically has thoughts about things she needs to accomplish. These thoughts may come up randomly or when she is reminded by something. Use the following example:

For example, when you are in the bathroom, you may notice that the faucet drips and remember that you wanted to fix that. But as soon as you are out of the bathroom, you forget about it. You only remember the next time you are in the bathroom, and then you feel badly because it never seems to get done. There may be lots of these little things that can add up.

Using an Organizer

For people who begin having problems with fatigue, thinking and memory, or increased physical impairment, the use of an organizer, a PDA, a calendar on a mobile phone, or an iCalendar (such as through www.google.com/calendar, available on the Web for free) can be the most effective tool for keeping track of all the different aspects of life. It is also helpful for allocating time to do important things. Let the patient know that people who cope effectively with these problems almost always use such an organizer.

The organizer can serve many different functions. Explain that it can help with planning and organization, which, in turn, can help a person be more effective and get more done. It can also serve as a memory aid.

Address Book

Encourage the patient to keep names, addresses, phone numbers, and birthdays in an alphabetized section of her organizer. This way, she can have all the information she needs in one place.

Instructions

Organizers often have a section for long-term instructional information. Electronic organizers also usually have a section for notes. Encourage the patient to periodically write down needed information. She might also want to include directions for places she does not visit frequently, or instructions for operating a piece of equipment she uses only once in a while.

To-Do Lists

Tell the patient that keeping to-do lists is critically important to managing memory problems. Remind her that MS can affect all areas of her life: work, home, relationships, and herself. Explain that some people like to keep four separate lists, one for each area; other people keep one list, but check off which area each item is for. You may say something like the following:

> *This way, you can be sure you are taking care of all areas of your life. Sometimes, people tend to favor some areas of their lives while ignoring others. For example, a lot of people will keep lists for work and home, but neglect lists for friends and family or for themselves. But those areas are also very important for your well-being.*

Make the List

Instruct patients that the first thing to do is record everything they need to do without thinking about how important each thing is. Patients may feel overwhelmed and anxious when faced with a long list. Their lists may be more than they could possibly accomplish in one day. Explain that this is where prioritizing comes in.

Prioritize the List

Suggest the following coding system for prioritizing to-do lists.

1. Code something as a "1" if it is a task that must be done today before any other activity, such as mailing a tax return or making sure there is enough food in the house.

2. Basic items that you would like to get done after all your "1s" are completed should be coded as "2s." An example of a "2" might be balancing your checkbook.

3. Routine items that are less important and have no deadline should be coded as "3s." An example of a "3" might be cleaning out the storage area.

Work together with the patient to help her create her to-do list on the form provided in the workbook.

There may also be a to-do list in the patient's organizer. Encourage the patient to continually add to her list as she thinks of things she needs to do. As she finishes things, she can check them off. Explain that this system will help her keep track of things she still has to do and may also give her a sense of accomplishment for the completed items. Patients may also prefer to create a new list every week.

Realistic Daily Goals

Let the patient know that one very important rule in planning her day is to plan only a limited number of to-do's. She should plan only an amount she thinks she can accomplish in that day. Planning too much and completing too little can lead to feelings of defeat, which, in turn, makes one less motivated to plan anything for the next day. Most people overestimate the amount of things they can accomplish. Therefore, in the beginning, it is better to plan too little than to plan too much. Experience will determine how many things the patient can accomplish in one day.

Planning Your Day

It doesn't matter when patients do it, but suggest that they may want to pick one time every day to go over their organizer and make their plans.

Using the patient's prioritized to-do list, help the patient create a plan for the next day using the Planning My Day form in the workbook.

Planning for Bigger Jobs

Explain that everyone has big tasks to do that can sometimes seem overwhelming—things like cleaning out a basement or sorting through boxes of old records. These kinds of things are often very hard to start and very difficult to complete. They are hard to start because they can seem so overwhelming that we don't know where to begin and may feel defeated even before we start. They can be difficult to finish because even after a lot of work, we may feel like we haven't made any progress.

Break Jobs Down into Small Parts

Tell the patient that the key to tackling big, overwhelming tasks is to break them up into smaller tasks that are more easily completed. You may want to say the following to illustrate:

> *For example, cleaning out the garage might seem like an overwhelming task. However, if you break it up into smaller pieces that are easier to complete, you will begin seeing progress. Rather than putting "clean the storage area" on your to-do list, you might break it down into five, ten, or even twenty pieces. For example, "clean off left half of the work bench" could be the first piece.*

Have the patient identify a big task that has been overwhelming for her and help her break it down into manageable tasks. Use the My Overwhelming Tasks form in the workbook.

Using the Calendar as a "Tickler File"

Another problem that interferes with completing tasks is that a patient might get started with things, but then forget to follow up. Encourage the patient to use the calendar in her organizer as a "tickler file." Explain that this means she makes appointments with herself in the future to follow up on items or tasks. You may want to use the following examples:

> *If you call your dentist to make an appointment and get a recording that the office is closed for a week, make a note to yourself in your calendar to call again the following week. If you have dropped your watch off for repair and it should be done in 3 days, make a note to yourself to call to follow up.*

Obstacles that Interfere with Planning and Organization

Having Attention and Concentration Problems

People often find at the end of the day that they haven't accomplished the things they set out to do and are not sure why. Frequently, this is an indication of problems with attention and concentration. Many people with MS find that they have no trouble concentrating on one task. Explain, however, that we may sometimes find that everyday activities absorb all of our attention, leaving us little time for tasks we had planned. You may want to say something like the following:

> *For example, you may have set aside a certain time to balance your checkbook. Then someone comes along and asks you a question, which perhaps leads to a conversation, and soon you are doing something else. At the end of the day, your checkbook is still not balanced, and you start feeling like you can't get anything done.*

> *Of course, it would be better if you only had one thing to do at a time. Then you could focus and complete the task. Unfortunately most of the time, you are probably trying to juggle multiple tasks. In addition, most likely, you have family, friends, and coworkers who also compete for your attention. It is therefore important to assert your needs. So, if people interrupt you while you are working on your checkbook, you may need to ask them to put off their question until after you have finished.*

Many people feel uncomfortable asking not to be disturbed. Or sometimes people find when they ask for such things it leads to conflict. Tell patients that if this is the case, they'll find some helpful tips in module 1 on communication (chapter 7 of the workbook).

Having "Bad MS Days"

People with MS sometimes just have days where they have a lot more fatigue than usual, or they notice that they can't think as clearly as they normally do. Often, people know when they get up that it is going to be "one of those days." Tell patients, in that case, it is better to take stock of the energy they have, and their cognitive abilities for the day, and change their plans accordingly. They might want to take a few minutes over breakfast to review the day ahead and make the necessary changes. Emphasize that it is better to adjust their plans in advance than allow them to be adjusted by MS.

> *Just pushing ahead with plans that you are not capable of completing or can only complete at great cost to yourself is letting your MS get the better of you. Planning around your capacity for that day leaves you in the driver's seat.*

Having a Lot of "Bad MS Days" in a Row

If patients notice that they have to adjust their schedules down every day for more than a week, then it is time to consider whether they are expecting too much of themselves. Have patients go back over their organizers and see if they have been increasing the amount they expect of themselves. If so, they have been experiencing a little "mission creep" which occurs when plans for oneself grow slowly but steadily until one can no longer do them.

If the patient has not been increasing her plans, but notices that she is just more fatigued and has a harder time cognitively over a period of a week or more, she may be having an exacerbation. Discuss this further if needed, and have the patient consider calling her neurologist.

Having Negative Emotional Reactions

Let patients know that there are always times when tasks on their list do not get completed. Often people either get frustrated with themselves and feel stressed and overwhelmed or just try to ignore the fact that they were unable to complete the task. Neither of these reactions is very helpful.

Problems with motivation may partially contribute to these uncompleted tasks. If the patient's difficulty with motivation is so great that she cannot get things done, consider whether or not she is scheduling enough enjoyable activities. Explain to the patient if her schedule is all work and no play, she will make herself unhappy and unmotivated. In chapter 3 of the workbook, the patient learned about how to include enjoyable activities in her schedule. Revisit this topic as needed (see chapter 5 on positive activities).

If a task doesn't get completed, encourage patients to look at this as an opportunity to see how they might be able to improve their organizational system. At the end of the day, they might want to look at each item they did not complete, and run through a brief analysis to see what may have interfered with task completion. This analysis will increase awareness of interfering factors and help with future problem solving. The workbook includes the following checklist:

- **Got distracted**

   Who or what distracted you?

   If this happens again, what could you do differently?

- **Didn't have time**

   What were you doing at that time?

   Did something else take too long?

   Did you have too much scheduled that day?

   Was it something unforeseen that came up?

   What can you do tomorrow to keep this specific problem from happening again?

- **It just seemed like too much to do**
  Can you break it into smaller components?
  What are those smaller components?

- **I did not have everything I needed to get this done**
  What did you need to complete this task?
  How can you prepare better to avoid this in the future?

Other Organization Tips

In our experience, patients who start experiencing cognitive impairment start having problems with mail and bills, as well as a growing amount of clutter and disorganization in the house. Review the following organizational tips to discuss how patients might gain more control over their household. Encourage patients to evaluate other areas of their homes and lives that need more organizational attention.

Do It Now!

Encourage patients to do things as soon as possible, preferably now, to avoid forgetting. Sometimes we may think we'll remember to do something later only to simply forget all about it. If patients cannot do the task immediately, tell them to write it in their to-do list right away.

Also, caution patients not to let things pile up so much that the sheer number of tasks to be done becomes overwhelming. For example, it is generally easier to zip through five pieces of mail every day than to try to plod through 120 pieces of mail once a month.

Bunching

Explain that, generally, while it is better not to let things pile up, for some tasks, it may be better to bunch them all together. For example, rather than paying bills one by one as they come in, it may be better to set up a folder for unpaid bills. When bunching tasks, patients should keep everything they are bunching in one designated place. This way, when they want to pay their bills, they will all be in one place instead of scattered about the house.

Put Things in the Same Place

Ask patients how much of their time they spend looking for things. They should make sure everything has its place and that they always put it back there. This task may be difficult because everyone in the patient's house has to agree to participate in this. Suggest that the patient, along with the other members of his household, can think of each object in the house as having its own "parking place." The patient can set up a rule in which if anyone in his household displaces anything, she can give them a "parking ticket." In this way, everyone in the household can work together to be consistent about keeping things in a designated spot.

Set Up "Work Centers"

Ask patients to think about the places in their homes where they spend time. These might include the bathroom, the kitchen, or maybe an office. They should make sure each of these "centers" is comfortable. For example, is the lighting adequate? Do they have good seating, and a good work surface? Patients should make sure they have everything they need and set things up so they don't have to run around looking for things.

Whenever patients find themselves carrying something back and forth, have them think about whether or not they should purchase another one. Duplicate supplies or equipment can be helpful so patients don't have to go back and forth. For example, if the patient needs a pair of scissors in the kitchen and on her desk, she may want to have two pairs. If she has two floors in her home, she might want a vacuum cleaner on each floor.

Organize Your Household

Sometimes, when a patient starts getting organized, people around her start depending on her to remind them. Tell the patient to be careful that this does not happen. Suggest setting up a household calendar on or near the refrigerator. The patient can inform those who live with her that a given event will not happen unless it is entered on the household calendar. For example, if someone needs a ride to the game next Saturday, it needs to be on the calendar. One way to jazz it up would be to use a different color pen for each person.

Mail

One of the most frequent things people lose at home is mail. Somehow the mail may wind up in a dozen different places. Suggest setting up a mail center that can be a plastic or wooden bin into which the mail is put every day. The patient can set up a time to process the contents of that bin every day. When a piece of mail is taken out of the mail center, it is a good idea to immediately sort it and either throw it away or place it in a folder for unpaid bills. Warn the patient against letting the mail "wander" around the house.

Phone Messages

Ask patients if their phone messages get lost (or written on the back of a pizza box). Recommend the patient buy a supply of Post-it Notes® and use one color for phone messages. Advise the patient to keep a supply next to the phone along with a pen. Also suggest creating a "message center"—one spot where all phone messages are left. The message center should be next to the phone. Explain that the Post-it Notes® are handy because the patient can transfer the messages into her organizer (if it is a paper and pencil organizer) without having to write them down immediately. If the call is not returned by the end of the day, she should transfer it to her to-do list.

Cutting Down on Distractions

If patients are having difficulty with getting back on task after being distracted, help them find ways to reduce distractions. Consider some of the following:

- Find a quiet place to work. Ask your boss for accommodations if necessary.

- Turn off the phone for periods of time, to avoid distraction. At work, roll it over to voicemail. At home, turn off the ringer. (Make a note to remind yourself to turn it on if necessary.)

- Keep people from bothering you. Put a "Do Not Disturb" sign outside your office or cubicle. At home, ask your family not to bother you—use a sign there too, if it helps.

- Turn off radios and TVs. Buy ear plugs if you cannot reduce distracting noises.

Consistency Is Key!

Having an organizer and a lot of strategies will never help if patients do not use them. Emphasize that it takes some time every day to truly make progress in gaining control over one's life. Ideally, patients may want to take 5–10 min at the end of every day to review the day, check off and update items on their to-do list, check their calendar and plan the following day, look at what did not get done that day, and analyze why. Have patients set aside one specific time each day for this review. They should let everyone in the household know that is their time for organization. In the morning, they should review the coming day. Encourage patients to keep the organizer with them at all times, as they may come to rely heavily on it.

Homework

While you should always be specific in assigning homework, it is of particular importance for people who have organizational problems. Determine a specific time of day and place where the patient will look at her organizer, prioritize events, and plan. If the patient only wants to do this one time a day, suggest that she plan in the morning. If the patient prefers the evening, she can try that as an experiment. Whichever it is, plan it. If there are additional topics to be assigned, be specific in those assignments as well.

✎ Have the patient begin using an organizer (electronic or otherwise). The patient should schedule a time each day to review the previous day and update the coming day.

✎ Have the patient create her to-do list using the form in the workbook.

✎ Have the patient complete the Planning My Day form in the workbook.

✎ Have the patient complete the My Overwhelming Tasks form in the workbook.

✎ Have the patient use the checklist in the workbook when she has trouble completing planned activities.

✎ Assign workbook reading as appropriate.

✎ Discuss any assignments relevant to the patient's goals.

Module 7 · Self-Injection Anxiety Counseling (SIAC)

(Corresponds to chapter 13 of the workbook)

Overview

This module is designed for patients who have needle anxiety and who rely on self-injection for the management of their illness. Many of these patients are not phobic enough to prevent them from receiving medications when someone else injects them, but anxiety interferes with their ability to self-inject. There are several reasons why it is useful for patients to learn to self-inject. Patients who do not self-inject are more likely to discontinue the medication (Mohr, Boudewyn, Likosky, Levine, & Goodkin, 2001). The people on whom they rely may not always be available or may not be dependable. People who rely on clinics to perform the injection may become tired to having to go to the clinic on a regular basis. Some people may also have difficulty with the dependency that reliance on others brings.

In our experience, the vast majority of patients, who initially cannot self-inject because of psychological reasons, are able learn to do so within 6 weeks, some in only 1 or 2 weeks (Mohr, Cox, Epstein, & Boudewyn, 2002) (Mohr, Cox, & Merluzzi, 2005). This module is designed to be conducted in 6 weekly 50-min sessions. While some patients may have success earlier, many patients require this amount of time to both learn to self-inject and learn skills to maintain their abilities in the face of any potential future reemergence of anxiety.

Basic Information about Self-Injection Anxiety

Many patients who can receive injections without difficulty may experience phobic reactions when faced with the need to self-inject. We will refer to anxiety that prevents self-injection as "self-injection anxiety."

Two types of self-injections are commonly performed at home: subcutaneous (SC) injections and intramuscular (IM) injections. IM injections may prove more daunting for patients because of the length and gauge of the needle. In addition to the type of injection, the frequency and duration of the injection schedule may contribute to or help reduce phobic symptoms. Repeated exposure to a feared stimulus can reduce phobic symptoms. As such, frequent self-injection may facilitate habituation to self-injection, while longer intervals between injections may strengthen anxiety and phobic reactions, particularly following unpleasant injection experiences such as pain, bleeding, injection site reactions, or medication side effects. In other words, more frequent self-injections may allow patients to "get used to it." The consequences of self-injection may also serve to increase or decrease anxiety and phobic reactions. In the case of self-injection for migraine or sexual dysfunction, the resulting relief from migraine pain or the pleasure associated with improved sexual functioning may reinforce self-injection. For patients who use medications that are primarily preventive or have side effects, the unpleasant injection experiences and aftermath may be the primary experience. These patients may be more vulnerable to anxiety and phobic reactions, particularly following an unpleasant injection experience.

Psychiatric Comorbidities

The small literature on the relationship between psychiatric disturbance and self-injection anxiety suggests that people with self-injection anxiety are at greater risk for depression and other types of phobias (Mollema, Snoek, Ader, Heine, & van der Ploeg, 2001). Thus, practitioners working with injection phobic patients should be alert to such comorbidities. The presence of other depressive or anxiety disorders may complicate the treatment by reducing adherence to treatment procedures (DiMatteo, Lepper, & Croghan, 2000; Mohr et al., 1996; Mohr et al., 1997). For example, depressed individuals may lack the motivation to carry through on homework, while patients with other anxiety disorders may be too overwhelmed to participate constructively. If other psychiatric problems are interfering, the injection counselor should refer the person for treatment of these disorders before proceeding with injection training.

Vasovagal Responses

Vasovagal responses are another potential complicating factor. A vasovagal response is characterized by an episode of a racing heartbeat and drop in blood pressure, either immediately preceding or concurrent with the injection. This may result in the patient passing out (called syncope), or can produce feelings of faintness or dizziness, pallor, queasiness or nausea, depersonalization, and ringing in the ears. Recent estimates of the occurrence of vasovagal responses in injection phobic patients range from 25% to 37% (Antony, Brown, & Barlow, 1997; De Jongh et al., 1998; Kleinknecht, Thorndike, & Walls, 1996). Anticipatory fear of vasovagal response appears to be much more prevalent. Vasovagal responses are almost always quite brief and benign, although there have been case reports of ventricular fibrillation, myocardial infarction, and cerebral infarction in patients with blood injury illness (BII) and severe vascular disease following exposure to injection or venipuncture (Hamilton, 1995).

Vasovagal responses may complicate the treatment of self-injection anxiety. Generally, the most efficacious treatment for phobias is behavioral exposure therapy, which involves repeatedly exposing the patient to the feared stimulus. However, for patients with severe vasovagal reactions, reactions may persist despite frequent exposure. One treatment outcome study suggests that patients with a history of vasovagal responses may be less likely to respond successfully to exposure training alone than phobia patients without vasovagal responses (Hellstrom & Ost, 1996). We have found that our treatment is effective for vasovagal patients.

Therapist Note

■ *For safety, vasovagal patients should always remain seated or lying down during treatment. If they are seated, they should be seated such that if they lose balance or consciousness, they will not fall or be harmed. We recommend greater relative focus on managing unhelpful thoughts about injection, compared to relaxation, because increased physiological relaxation may contribute to the sharp decrease in blood pressure that can lead to unconsciousness. For these patients, a mild stimulant such as caffeine may also be helpful prior to injection. Beta-blockers may also be helpful. If relaxation is used, it is best to focus that relaxation specifically on the injection site. If possible, it is helpful to teach the patient to increase muscle tone in the neck and shoulders (to maintain blood pressure) while increasing relaxation at the injection site.* ■

For any patients with a history of fainting or feeling faint, it is reassuring to demonstrate that, should they faint, they will not hurt themselves. Have them practice injecting in an infusion chair or some other comfortable seating arrangement where they cannot fall over. Remind them that even in the very worst case scenario—they pass out while injecting—they will not be harmed, they will not bleed to death, nothing catastrophic will happen, and they will only remain unconscious for a few seconds.

For patients who have a history of feeling faint when seeing blood, instruction in proper site selection to avoid veins and creating a hierarchy around blood (i.e. look at a drop of blood on the gauze after bleeding has stopped after injection, then waiting a second before applying the gauze to see if there is bleeding, etc.) is very helpful.

Cognitive Impairment

This model has been used successfully with patients who have mild to moderate cognitive impairment. Except in the most severe cases, cognitive impairment alone should not prevent a patient from benefiting from this model. However, when working with a patient who has cognitive impairment, you should be sure to provide additional aids and cues. These patients will benefit from the structure the workbook provides. Writing down homework assignments and providing written direction will also be helpful. If the patient is willing, involving the person who has been giving the injections can also be helpful. This person can help the patient remember to practice homework and bring the workbook to meetings. If your patient has problems with attention, you can have him choose the relaxation exercise he prefers, and then ask him to practice only that one exercise. Finally, when working with people with cognitive impairment, be sure a reminder system for the injections is in place. As the patient learns to self-inject, you do not want this newfound independence to result in missed doses because of forgetfulness or lack of organization.

SESSION 1

Materials Needed

- Copy of patient workbook
- Injection hierarchy form
- Relaxation script

Outline

- Establish rapport and goals for treatment
- Review the anxiety response
- Introduce cognitive-behavioral therapy (CBT) for self-injection
- Introduce use of hierarchies
- Introduce relaxation training

Goals for Treatment

The most common impediments to treatment are anxiety, nervousness, and embarrassment. Spending just a few moments reassuring patients that their concerns and fears are common and that Self-Injection Anxiety Counseling (SIAC) is an effective treatment for injection anxiety can help them calm down significantly. Patients who initially were able to self-inject but who are now having difficulty may be particularly embarrassed and feel as if they will be perceived as a failure, "wimpy," or not invested in their treatment. Saying something like the following may help normalize the patient's feelings:

> *Having difficulty with injections is a very common problem. Self-injecting is even more difficult for most people. We spend a lot of our time ensuring that we don't ever get into a situation where we are intentionally breaking our skin or sticking ourselves with something sharp as it is an unnatural thing to do, and it's perfectly normal to have difficulty with it. You certainly aren't the first person with this problem!*

Some patients may also cope with their anxiety by presenting as somewhat withdrawn or very businesslike. Establishing a warm and accepting atmosphere can help draw patients like this out and allow them to discuss their anxiety more openly.

Some patients may be very clear that their primary goal is to self-inject, and that they expect they will be able to achieve this goal. However, it's also common for patients to say that they are pretty sure they will never be able to self-inject, and that they only hope to decrease the anxiety they experience while they are undergoing an injection. Through the use of this program, most patients will be able to self-inject. While it is important to help establish hope in patients, it is not necessary in the first session to convince them that they will be able to self-inject. In fact, if they have strong initial doubts, monitoring their doubt as it decreases can be a helpful aspect of therapy. Overcoming these doubts may lead to a greater sense of self-efficacy and pride after they are able to self-inject.

The Anxiety Response

The physiological anxiety response was described in a more detailed fashion as the stress response in module 4 on relaxation. Patients often have a good intuitive understanding of the physiological process of arousal they experience when self-injecting. It's a good idea to begin by reviewing this process with an example, such as the following, and explaining how this model will work within this process.

> *The anxiety response is a collection of physiological responses to a frightening and dangerous situation. Imagine that you are cleaning*

your garage, and as you take your hand down from a shelf, you realize that a large spider has crawled right onto your hand. Your body will have an emotional arousal response: you may scream a little, quickly brush your hand off, or quickly move away from the shelf. The emotional arousal response includes rapid breathing, increased heart rate, sweating, increased muscle tension, increased blood flow to the muscles and heart (and away from processes like digestion), release of adrenaline and other substances that cause arousal, and many other physiological processes. As you continued to clean your garage, you would probably be more alert and feel a little nervous when you couldn't see your hands. If something brushed against your fingers that felt like it might be a spider, you might jerk your hand back, feel your pulse race, or even feel dizzy. The anxiety response would be working to try to keep you safe. However, if you kept cleaning and didn't encounter any more spiders, eventually the anxiety response would start to fade away, and your body would be relaxed and calm.

Explain to the patient that what happens with injection anxiety is that an experience such as seeing a needle or self-injecting is associated with this anxiety response—our bodies start to respond to the cues of self-injecting as if we were in a life-threatening situation. Self-Injection Anxiety Counseling treatment breaks the association between the anxiety response and the act of self-injecting. It does this in several ways: by using the stress and mood management model to control one's thoughts and understand one's feelings, by practicing relaxation to gain more control over one's physiology, and by practicing the steps leading up to self-injecting slowly to gain confidence and control.

Make sure patients understand the anxiety model and ask them to apply it to their own lives. What physiological symptoms of anxiety do they experience? You can stress the role of slow, calm, deep breathing in relaxation, and stress that anxiety and relaxation are physiological opposites and cannot occur simultaneously. Remind patients that the goal of treatment is not to make anxiety completely disappear. First, this goal is likely unobtainable. Second, anxiety is a natural and important part of our experience. Instead, patients learn to control and keep their anxiety at manageable levels.

As in the other stress and mood management program modules, you and the patient will create the agenda collaboratively at the beginning of each session. Each session should include a rating of the patient's injection anxiety, regardless of whether the injection is administered by you, someone else, or ultimately by the patient.

Review of injection anxiety and homework will follow the agenda in subsequent sessions.

The Stress and Mood Management Model

Refer the patient to the stress and mood management model as it relates to injection anxiety (Figure M7.1)

Briefly review how the five components (cognition, emotion, physical, behavior, and social) are all continuously interacting with each other. These components are also involved in the anxiety reaction a person has when trying to self-inject. The person's body becomes physiologically aroused. The person experiences a feeling of fear, anxiety, or tension. The person may have thoughts such as "it's going to hurt" or "I'll never be able to do this." Behaviorally, the person may freeze up. As these components all interact with each other, a vicious cycle of anxiety can develop.

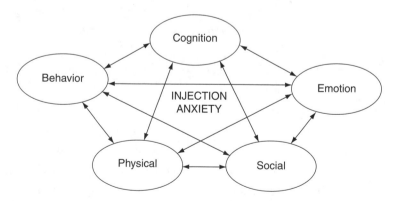

Figure M7.1

Stress and mood management model (injection anxiety).

Each component can feed on the others to increase a person's overall experience of anxiety. For example, if a person is afraid that the shot will hurt, he will experience the physical reactions associated with fear (e.g. tensing of the muscles). When the muscles are more tense, the injection becomes more painful. This could lead to the thought "it hurts even more than I thought it would," which increases the person's fear, which increases muscle tension, and makes the next shot more painful. Explain to the patient that we can intervene at each of the components to some degree, and reverse the spiral. By monitoring unhelpful thoughts about injecting and changing them, we can gain control over that component. By practicing relaxation, we can control our physiological responses to injecting. By making changes in the environment, we can make the process of injecting less anxiety-provoking. By making changes in our behavior, we can make the process of injecting less anxiety-provoking and less painful.

Have the patient recall a time when injecting or trying to inject was difficult for him and ask the following questions:

- "What kinds of bodily sensations did you experience at the time?" ("Maybe you noticed your breathing becoming faster or shallower, your hand shaking, or your heart racing?")

- "What kinds of thoughts did you have about yourself as a result?" (Common thoughts are "It will hurt," "I will injure myself, hit a nerve, hit a bone," etc.)

- "What kind of mood were you in as a result?" ("Anxious or fearful?")

- "What kinds of behavior(s) did you engage in or stop engaging in as a result of the experience, your thoughts about the experience, and your mood resulting from the experience?"

- "What does this mean for the relationship you have with the person who is administering the injection?" (Some patients feel dependent. Others feel grateful. If receiving the injection positively affects the relationship, acknowledge this and ask if there are other ways these positive aspects can be preserved.)

The Subjective Units of Distress (SUDS) Rating

One of the first things the patient should do is rank her anxiety on a scale from 0 to 100, with 0 meaning no anxiety at all, and 100 meaning the worst anxiety the patient has ever experienced. It's important that patients understand this, because you will be asking them to use this skill to rank their anxiety as you practice relaxation skills, as they develop their Injection Hierarchy, as they practice the items on the hierarchy, and as they complete Unhelpful Thought Diaries. By monitoring their rankings throughout treatment, you can use this information to chart patients' progress.

Introduction to the Use of Hierarchies

The key to learning to self inject is to start slow and take small steps. Encourage the patient to identify other situations in her life where this strategy has been successful, such as learning how to play a sport, learning how to use a computer, or mastering any complex and potentially intimidating task.

Ask the patient to think about all the steps that lead up to the injection process in order of difficulty, starting with the easiest, and assign them SUDS anxiety ratings using the My Injection Hierarchy form in chapter 12 of the workbook. Examples of questions to ask the patient include:

- "How much anxiety do you have preparing for the injection?"

- "How much anxiety do you have preparing your leg to receive the shot?"

- "How much anxiety do you have around actually injecting?"

- "How much anxiety would you have about depressing the plunger after I have inserted the needle into your leg?"

- "How much anxiety do you have about observing me giving you the shot?"

Ask as many sample questions like this as needed to help your patient generate a variety of activities with different difficulty levels. For most patients, actually self-injecting will be rated as 100. You want your patient to generate a number of activities that range from a 20 or 30 on the difficulty scale up to 100. Patients can list actual physical activities, (e.g. looking at the needle, touching the needle, injecting an orange—oranges feel very close to administration of intramuscular injections), or mental activities (visualizing themselves injecting or visualizing the needle entering their skin).

Involvement of Person Doing Injections

Since this program of learning to self-inject typically takes 3–6 weeks, patients will continue to receive injections for a while. If you are able to give the patient injections, it is often helpful to schedule the appointments so that you can administer them and work with the patient more closely around the injection process. If the patient will continue to receive injections from someone else (e.g. a family member), it will be important to involve this person in the patient's treatment. Ideally, this person could also attend sessions. If not, the patient should work with the person doing the injection to accomplish items on her hierarchy.

Review the Use of Relaxation

The patient should have completed module 4 on relaxation prior to beginning SIAC. The purpose of relaxation training is to give your patients the ability to quickly and effectively relax when they are anxious. Encourage patients to practice controlled breathing techniques throughout the day, every day, as it will be very important for the exercises in this module that they are able to use breathing to control their anxiety, fear, and arousal associated with needles. Ideally, they should also practice a relaxation exercise at least once a day, every day, during the first few weeks of treatment. If there are limitations in achieving these goals, the counselor should problem solve with the patient to find a time of the day and a quiet environment that will allow the patient to practice at least a few times a week. If you have done relaxation training before with patients, you can use your own relaxation script.

Importance of Homework

Practicing at home helps generalize learning from the treatment sessions to their home environment, where they will in fact be giving themselves the majority of their injections. Ask patients what parts of the home assignments they think will be difficult to comply with, and help them find solutions to the problems around them. Remind them that although their anxiety may initially increase while they are doing this treatment, the end result will be the increased independence and feeling of self-confidence that accompanies successful self-injections.

Homework

✎ Have the patient read corresponding section of the workbook chapter.

✎ Have the patient practice relaxation daily.

✎ Have the patient practice controlled breathing when receiving injections and at other stressful moments over the week.

✎ Have the patient complete an injection hierarchy.

SESSION 2

Materials Needed

■ Copy of patient workbook

■ Injection hierarchy form

Outline

- Set the agenda and get SUDS rating

- Review homework

- Review injection hierarchy

- Practice first item on hierarchy

- Introduce systematic desensitization

- Assign homework

Setting the Agenda

Begin the session by setting the agenda with the patient. It should include a review of the homework and a review of the hierarchy. It should also include any issues the patient is having that are relevant—any questions about technique, medications, disease, or any other issues. Get a SUDS rating for the weekly injections, and note who performed the injections. Note any changes in SUDS rating since last week; patients may feel more confident and less anxious. Also be sure to ask the patient what he wants to include in the agenda.

Review of Homework

The patient should have continued to build upon the hierarchy you introduced in the first session, as well as practiced relaxation and deep breathing. Discuss any problems that came up in completing the homework.

Review of Injection Hierarchy

You may want to help the patient expand the number of activities on the hierarchy to include a wide range of ratings. Suggest activities such as watching a video (many pharmaceutical companies provide videotaped instruction on how to self-inject) or practicing injecting an orange, holding the needle with the cap on, holding the needle with the cap off, holding the needle above the skin, etc. Even if the patient says that these are not difficult to do, you might consider assigning them a hierarchy rating. It is helpful for patients to see the range of injection-related activities and the range of levels of distress. However when selecting activities for the patient to practice, begin with experiences that have some minimal level of difficulty for the patient, but are not so anxiety-provoking that they overwhelm the patient and result in a failure experience. The experience of beginning with easier items and slowly moving to the more difficult items in the hierarchy should provide a success experience and increase self-efficacy. For most patients, starting with items that rank between a 30 and 50 on the SUDS scale should arouse sufficient anxiety to provide a challenge, but not so much anxiety that the chance of success is reduced. As the patient progresses through the hierarchy, periodically have the patient rerate the items, as very often patients will reconsider the difficulty level of items as they move through the hierarchy.

First Item on Hierarchy and Relaxation Practice

Once you and the patient have identified the steps in the hierarchy, select the first item for practice. This item should be at a SUDS level of 30 or above. Have the patient perform the feared activity in session. When he notices his anxiety rising, immediately stop the activity and begin a brief relaxation exercise:

> *Begin to focus on your breath, taking slow, calm, and deep relaxing breaths. Become aware of any tension you are holding in your body, any feelings of nervousness, and with each slow, deep, relaxing breath, allow your body to relax and become calm. Focus on your breath, taking slow, calm, deep breaths. Feel the sense of peaceful relaxation increase with each calming breath. Become aware of any thoughts you're having, any feelings. Be aware of them, but just let them go, just push them aside. What's important right now is that feeling of calm, cool relaxation that you can feel throughout your body. Notice the relaxation in your face, your shoulders, your neck (anywhere else the*

patient has tension). Just relax, and feel your deep calm breaths, and the cool, peaceful sense of relaxation, confidence, and comfort. When you're ready, you can take that sense of calm and relaxation with you as you open your eyes.

Once the patient's anxiety has returned to a low level, instruct him to begin the activity again. When his anxiety begins to rise, again stop the patient and conduct the relaxation exercise. Repeat this process for 20–30 min, unless the patient's anxiety remains at a constant low level with less practice. If this is the case, then you should move to the next item on the hierarchy, repeating the same process.

The goal is for the patient to be able to monitor his anxiety and implement the relaxation process himself over the course of the next week. For the final in-session practice, have the patient identify when he is becoming too anxious, and do the relaxation exercise himself.

Systematic Desensitization

Systematic desensitization has repeatedly been shown to be helpful in overcoming anxiety and phobias. If the patient is reluctant to use guided imagery that includes a description of self-injection, work with the patient to choose an imagery that includes at least an item from the injection hierarchy. Be sure you know many details about the context and environment where the patient will eventually perform the self-injection. The details may be these: what does the room look like, will there be music or other sounds, smells, what does the chair feel like where the patient will sit, etc? These details are useful in developing a relaxed, hypnotic state, and make the experience more realistic for the patient. Agree on a signal that the patient can give you if the anxiety becomes too great, such as lifting an index finger. Then use a relaxation exercise to put the patient into a relaxed state. While the patient is relaxed, use guided imagery to walk the patient through the entire injection process, up to the agreed upon point. Incorporate the sights, sounds, smells, and feelings of the environment where the patient would be performing the injection. If the patient signals anxiety, halt the imagery and begin using a relaxing exercise. Ask the patient to signal (e.g. lower the index finger) when he feels relaxed again and then continue with the injection imagery. This type of systematic desensitization can be very useful in reducing anxiety associated with the injection process and increasing self-confidence in one's ability to successfully complete a self-injection.

Homework

✐ Have the patient continue relaxation practice.

✐ Have the patient continue with hierarchy. Collaborate with the patient to choose items to practice over the week.

✐ Have the patient complete Unhelpful Thought Diaries at the time of injection and when he performs his injection hierarchy activities.

✐ Encourage the patient to reward himself for his successes!

SESSION 3

Materials Needed

- Copy of patient workbook
- Injection hierarchy form
- Challenging Unhelpful Thoughts Diary

Outline

- Set the agenda, get SUDS rating, and review homework
- Discuss unhelpful thoughts
- Assign homework

Setting the Agenda, SUDS Rating, and Homework Review

Begin by setting the agenda, getting a SUDS rating, and discussing the homework from last week. Discuss the patient's independent practice with the hierarchy.

Unhelpful Thoughts

Review the stress and mood management model presented in the first week of treatment. You may want to say something like the following:

> *Very often, when we're in a situation that's anxiety-provoking, our automatic thoughts are distinctly unhelpful. For example, some people have the automatic thought "this is going to hurt" when they see the needle. They persist in having this thought despite the experience of painless injections at times.*

Review any Unhelpful Thought Diaries the patient brought into the session. Some patients will be able to identify unhelpful thoughts easily without any help. Other patients may need to be exposed to anxiety-provoking stimuli, such as holding the needle, in order to identify any unhelpful thoughts. As the patient's anxiety rises, help him to put into words any thoughts he is having. Write down the unhelpful thoughts as the patient identifies them. Remind the patient that these thoughts don't need to make any sense or be rational. Some patients also have unhelpful mental images, such as the needle vanishing into their leg or breaking off. Being accepting and nonjudgmental of these fears will help patients confront them and express them. Help patients expand on these thoughts to get to the assumptions and beliefs behind them.

Some common unhelpful thoughts include:

- "It will hurt."

- "I can't do this."

- "I will mess up the injection and hurt myself somehow (inject into vein, inject air bubbles, damage muscle)."

- "I will freeze and be unable to inject."

- "I will panic."

- "This makes having my illness more real."

- "This means I can't deny I have this disease."

- "This means my disease is taking over my life."

- "I can't believe how much of a wimp I'm being."

- "I'm making a big deal out of nothing."

- "I should just be able to tough this out."

Allow the patient also to express intrusive and anxiety-provoking mental images. It is important that you accept patients' thoughts empathetically and without judgment. Saying something like "I can see how that might make you feel more anxious" helps draw the connection between the thought and anxiety, and also helps patients feel understood.

As the patient identifies his thoughts, work with him to complete a Challenging Unhelpful Thoughts Diary. For each unhelpful thought, help the patient identify the feelings and emotions that develop as a result of the thought (e.g. thinking one will damage oneself as a result of the injection can lead to fear, thinking of oneself as a wimp can lead to embarrassment, etc.). Have the patient assign a 0–10 rating to the strength of his belief in the thought, and have him assign a 0–10 rating to the strength of the emotion it produces.

Review common negative thought patterns (see chapter 6 for more information and descriptions of the types of cognitive distortions).

Name-calling: For example, calling oneself a "wimp" for not being able to self-inject is name-calling.

"Should" statements: For example, a lot of people think they "should" be able to inject themselves with no anxiety, or they "should not" be having this kind of difficulty.

Disqualifying the positive: For example, some people may focus on the fact that they are still having trouble with injections 3 weeks into therapy rather than focusing on the progress they have made.

All-or-nothing thinking: Very often, people will limit themselves to two opposite and extreme options, such as either being able to self-inject easily or not being able to take interferon medications at all.

Jumping to conclusions (the fortune teller error): Someone with this pattern might try to self-inject once, experience anxiety and be unable to do it, and then conclude "I'll never be able to do it; there's no reason to try again."

Catastrophizing: For example, "I had those flu-like symptoms last week after my shot, they are only going to get worse," "I'll have to stop the medication and my MS will start getting worse," "I'll be in a wheelchair within a month," etc.

Overinterpretion: For example, "I had some pain with the last injection. This is just never going to work."

Personalization: Patients with this pattern may worry a great deal about how you are responding to them—they may worry that their anxiety makes you uncomfortable or that you pity them or think they are "wimpy."

Emotional thinking: For example, if you feel afraid, you assume that there must be something dangerous happening. Or, if you feel embarrassed, you assume that you are doing something shameful.

Patients usually can identify at least one or two of these unhelpful thought patterns as personally applicable. Together with the patient, you can use the Challenging Unhelpful Thoughts Diary to combat the beliefs espoused by the unhelpful thought pattern. However, increased awareness alone can help patients avoid this pattern in the future. It can be helpful to have patients identify how this pattern impacts areas of their lives other than injecting as well, and to rehearse blocking the pattern by noticing it and using the positive self-statement "I will not allow this pattern to determine how I think right now" or "I will not allow this pattern or feeling to determine how I behave right now." You can also continue to refer back to the thought pattern as the patient experiences unhelpful thoughts throughout treatment. Some patients will identify events from their past that they feel contribute to these patterns, like identifying a past negative medical experience or noting that important people in their lives were critical when they demonstrated weakness. This is helpful if it allows the patient a better understanding of, and a greater control over his unhelpful thoughts, but it is not necessary for treatment to be successful.

Next, begin to question the unhelpful thoughts, starting with the ones that are rated less strongly by the patient. For some thoughts, particularly ones about making mistakes and hurting oneself, the process of questioning them is relatively easy. By providing patients with the information they need (e.g. explanation that it's impossible to hit a bone, instruction in proper technique, etc.), the strength of belief in these thoughts and the accompanying distressing emotions should quickly subside.

Some thoughts, such as "I'm being wimpy," can't really be considered "right" or "wrong." With thoughts like this, it can be very helpful to encourage patients to examine whether this thought helps them achieve their goals, rather than focusing on the "truth" of the thought. However, evidence against the thought can also be gathered—for example, identifying areas in the patient's life where he is brave, and noting the fact that many people on injectable medications, including medical professionals, have difficulty self-injecting. It can be helpful to ask patients what they would think if a good friend of theirs had a problem with injection—whether they would consider that person to be "wimpy." The process of developing rational responses to these thoughts is most effective if the patients take an active role and develop the majority of the rational responses themselves. Be sure to provide a great deal of support and encouragement.

Most patients have some thoughts that, by injecting, they are increasing the burden of having their illness or increasing the role that their illness has in their lives. This may be especially the case when patients have severe injection anxiety. Ask patients how much they worry about the shot and how much the shot interferes with their peace of mind. It is important to help patients differentiate between "the shot," a brief pricking sensation that lasts for less than 5 s; any side effects for the medication, which will pass; their anxiety about the shot, which may involve several hours of worrying each week; and their feelings and thoughts about having their illness. While it is helpful to talk about feelings and thoughts related to MS, it is important to help patients understand that the "the shot," a brief, albeit unpleasant, prick, actually helps control the disease and reduce the burden.

Homework

✎ Have the patient continue relaxation practice.

✎ Have the patient continue with hierarchy. Collaborate with the patient to choose items to practice over the week.

✎ Have the patient complete Challenging Unhelpful Thoughts Diaries at the time of injection and when he performs his injection hierarchy activities.

✎ Encourage the patient to reward himself for his successes!

SESSION 4

Materials Needed

- Copy of patient workbook
- Challenging Unhelpful Thoughts Diary
- Needle, syringe, and medication

Outline

- Set the agenda, get SUDS rating, and review homework
- Review unhelpful thought process
- Have the patient practice actual injection
- Assign homework

Setting the Agenda, SUDS Rating, and Homework Review

Begin by setting the agenda, getting a SUDS rating, and discussing the homework from last week. Discuss the patient's independent practice with the hierarchy.

The Actual Injection Process

Patients will usually remain quite anxious through their initial self-injection. It is important to remind them that this is normal, and that their goal is to make injecting manageable—it may never be pleasant. Stop as many times as is necessary in the injection process and practice relaxation to reduce anxiety. For IM injections, many patients who have difficulty with the "stabbing" aspect of injection find it much easier to lightly rest the tip of the needle against their skin, and then insert the needle from that position. Patients who are afraid of blood or pain can be reminded that by completing the steps of the injection process quickly, they will reduce these possible side effects. It is very important to provide lots of positive feedback as patients are actually injecting—remind them in an encouraging way to quickly insert the needle, depress the plunger, and remove the needle. Many patients will perform the process very slowly the first time, and the slower they go, the more likely they are to experience pain and anxiety.

Most patients experience a sense of pride and increased self-confidence after injecting. Some patients will feel so relieved that they become a little tearful. Many patients will say things like "that was so much easier than I thought it would be" or "that was no big deal." You should validate your patients for these realizations, while reminding them that learning to self-inject is anxiety-provoking for a lot of people, and their past anxiety was perfectly normal.

If patients are unable to complete the injection, having them do part of the injection process is still very helpful. You (or the person administering the injection) can insert the needle and have the patient depress the plunger and remove the needle, just as you have been doing with the hierarchies. Or, you can have the patient place his hand over the hand inserting the needle, and then have the patient take over once the needle is in. These intermediate steps bring the patient closer to completely self-injecting, model your good technique, and give the patient a sense of participation and empowerment. These steps can be initiated as early as the first session, if the patient feels able. Many patients, particularly those who were initially able to self-inject, get progressively slower during the injection process as their anxiety develops, and may take 30 or 45 s to insert the needle, and another 30 s to depress the plunger and remove the needle. This generally worsens pain and bruising, which increases anxiety. Modeling appropriate speed can be helpful for these patients. If your patient is injecting too slowly, having him practice inserting a needle quickly into firm surfaces at home, like the arm of a couch or a mattress, with a spare needle and syringe can be very helpful. It can also be helpful to demonstrate that you can place the needle just over the skin before piercing the skin.

Homework

✎ Have the patient continue relaxation practice. It is important that the patient maintains optimal control over his physiological arousal response.

✎ Have the patient continue with hierarchy. Collaborate with the patient to choose items to practice over the week.

✎ Have the patient complete Challenging Unhelpful Thoughts Diaries at the time of injection and when he performs his injection hierarchy activities.

✎ Encourage the patient to reward himself for his successes!

SESSION 5

Materials Needed

■ Needle, syringe, and medication

Outline

- Set the agenda, get SUDS rating, and review homework

- Have the patient practice actual injection

- Discuss transfer of learning to self-injecting at home

- Assign homework

Setting the Agenda, SUDS Rating, and Homework Review

Begin by setting the agenda, getting a SUDS rating, and discussing the homework from last week. Discuss the patient's independent practice with the hierarchy.

In-Session Self-Injection Practice

Many patients will have begun to self-inject in the fourth session or earlier, but some will have attempted it but been unable to, or will have scheduled the attempt for this session. The patients who successfully self-injected in session four should continue to self-inject with you in the remaining sessions, and they should continue to monitor their anxiety throughout the process. Any increases in anxiety throughout the process should be questioned, and the appropriate response to the cause of the anxiety should be taken, whether that's a relaxation exercise, education about injection technique, a Challenging Unhelpful Thoughts Diary, or other strategy. Most patients will quickly and easily self-inject the second time.

If your patient was unable to inject in session four, session five should focus on self-injecting. Using techniques such as hand-over-hand modeling can be very helpful. At each step of the injection process, it's important to identify the patient's thought that prevents successful injection and use relaxation and thought diaries to replace that thought with a more helpful one.

It's important to discuss differences between injecting at home and injecting in the clinic. The most important difference is your presence—while patients are being supervised, they can be sure that they aren't making any errors. Discussing any questions that remain about injection technique and reinforcing patients for their good technique is important to build confidence. You should help the patient identify a good injection routine for home. Help him choose a comfortable place to inject, and to identify optimal conditions for injection. Will the patient find relaxing music or aromatherapy candles comforting? Does he want someone else there, or will it be easier alone? What chair will he use? What day(s) will he inject, and what time of day? What schedule and type of remedies might the patient take for side effects, if they are a problem?

It is also very important that you encourage patients to reinforce themselves for injecting. They should build something nice for themselves into their injection routine. For example, some patients rent a movie the night after they inject, or cook a favorite meal (or have their partner cook a favorite meal). Other patients get a manicure, or buy a favorite snack for themselves. Remind your patients that they wouldn't hesitate to congratulate and celebrate the accomplishment of a child, friend, or an employee, and that they should extend the same courtesy to themselves.

Homework

- ✎ Have the patient continue relaxation practice.

- ✎ Have the patient continue with hierarchy. Collaborate with the patient to choose items to practice over the week.

- ✎ Have the patient complete Challenging Unhelpful Thoughts Diaries at the time of injection and when he performs his injection hierarchy activities.

- ✎ Encourage the patient to reward himself for his successes!

Materials Needed

- Any materials required, depending on the patient's progress (see previous sessions)

Outline

- Set the agenda, get SUDS rating, and review homework

- Have the patient practice actual injection

- Discuss relapse prevention

Setting the Agenda, SUDS Rating, and Homework Review

Begin by setting the agenda, getting a SUDS rating, and discussing the homework from last week. Discuss the patient's independent practice with the hierarchy.

Relapse Prevention

Identifying possible triggers for relapse is very important and can be very helpful. Helping patients to prepare for possible problems, including a painful injection, blood at the injection site, scheduling problems, or a feeling by the spouse or partner who had been doing the injections that the patient no longer needs them, is important. Use the workbook to help the patient make a plan for coping with any relapse triggers he can identify.

Discussing the differences between a lapse and a relapse is also helpful. The patient should plan that if he experiences a lapse—notices an increase in anxiety, notices a tendency to avoid the injection or rely on others to do the injection, etc.—he can intervene by contacting you and rereading the workbook, and redoing any exercises as necessary to regain a sense of confidence around injecting. Stress to the patient that it is much easier to intervene early in the process, rather than waiting until self-injecting becomes terribly anxiety-provoking or impossible.

For patients who can identify many potential triggers, you may wish to schedule a booster session a month or two after the last session to help cope with any problems that arise.

Module 8 *Ending Treatment and Maintaining Gains*

(Corresponds to chapter 14 of the workbook)

Materials Needed

- Copy of patient workbook
- Stress Management Plan form
- Weekly Check-In sheet

Outline

- Set the agenda
- Rate the patient's stress/distress level
- Review homework
- Introduce maintaining gains
- Review what the patient has learned
- Discuss the patient's reaction to ending weekly meetings and ending therapy overall
- Guide the patient through the steps of developing a stress management plan
- Assign homework

Therapist Note

■ *Note that this chapter will guide the final three sessions. You are not expected to complete the entire chapter in one session. Indeed, it is important to allow the patient time to adjust to maintenance. However, it is important to get through the self-monitoring check-ins so that the patient can practice this in the following week. It is a good idea to space out the final sessions initially with 2 weeks between sessions. Some patients may also like to increase this to 3 or 4 weeks between sessions.* ■

Overview

The final three sessions of the stress and mood management program should be devoted to termination and maintenance issues. This involves the same components which need to be incorporated into the basic structure of each session: (a) set an agenda; (b) review homework; (c) select at least one topic to work on in depth; (d) summarize; (e) set up a new homework assignment; and (f) do mutual feedback. But the patient should take the lead on these.

If it seems reasonable, let the patient know at the beginning of the session that she will be taking a greater role in running the remaining sessions, to help make sure the skills she learned stick.

■ Agenda: Explain how to set a collaborative agenda (get input from the therapist, prioritize, and summarize).

■ Rate distress.

■ Homework: Explain that the patient should tell you how the homework went, and maybe ask questions if any came up, or if she had difficulties completing anything.

Maintaining Gains

Inform patients that they are now coming to the end of the weekly meetings. During these weekly meetings, they have been talking about and practicing stress management skills, including identifying and challenging unhelpful ways of thinking, using relaxation to control the anxiety response, enhancing social support, planning and noticing positive things that happen, and other coping strategies. As they move into the next phase of the stress management program, patients will focus on maintaining the changes that they have made. Before therapy ends, however, you want to make sure that the changes patients want to maintain are well-integrated into their lives. To do this, together you will look back over what they have learned and what changes they have made up until now, and look forward to what they can do in the future. You will begin spacing out therapy visits to give patients time to practice implementing their plan to maintain gains. This chapter is divided into two parts:

1. Looking Back: Reviewing What Has Been Learned

2. Looking Forward: Developing a Stress Management Plan

Looking Back: Reviewing What Has Been Learned

Have the patient refer back to the Goal and Action Plan Worksheet(s) she created in the first 2 weeks of the program. Identify any other additional goals that were developed during the therapy and may not have been captured in a goals sheet. Review them with the following questions (space is provided in the workbook to write answers):

1. What was your goal (or goals) for the program? (Include both those for which the patient made a goal sheet, and those for which she did not.)

2. To what degree do you think that you have met this goal/these goals? Was it a complete success? Partial success? No success at all?

3. To the degree that each goal was not achieved, what got in the way? What could you do differently?

4. What helped you make the changes you did make?

5. What are some of the specific skills you have learned? Particularly focus on those skills you believe will be useful to you in the future for: managing stressful situations, transforming negative thoughts into more helpful ones, turning negative moods into more positive moods.

It might be useful to review the stress and mood management model— first introduced in chapter 3—as a way of reminding the patient of the various skills covered in the program. Have the patient note the skills she has learned in each of these areas:

- Behavioral skills (Doing things)

- Cognitive skills (Changing my thinking)

- Communication/Relationship skills

For each of the three areas, identify the skills learned, discuss when they are useful (e.g. triggers), and what the positive (and negative) outcomes are. Have the patient describe specific concrete examples of when and how these skills have been helpful.

Common Reactions to Ending the Weekly Meetings (and Ending Overall)

There are a variety of common reactions people may experience as the weekly meetings end. Some people may feel relief at not having to come every week. Sometimes people anticipate missing having a place to check in, or maybe even missing the regular meetings with the therapist. Others are worried about setbacks. And it is also common for people to look forward to having the extra time that has been devoted to the weekly meetings.

Discuss what kinds of reactions the patient has noticed as she anticipates the format changing to a monthly rather than weekly meeting. During the final sessions, we encourage discussions with the patient about (1) what ending therapy means, (2) the patient's ideas about what was more helpful and what was less helpful during treatment, and (3) the patient's feelings about the therapist as a person. Talking directly about these issues helps create a more positive ending, and will give the patient a sense of closure that is very important. You can also encourage the patient to complete the Unhelpful Thoughts Diaries (UTDs), or use the UTD format to help the patient explore her thoughts and feelings around ending therapy.

Another topic that may come up at this point in time is whether or not the patient should join a self-help group or a support group of some kind in order to stay in contact with other people who have had similar problems and gain support from them. This is an important issue that should be talked about frankly and thoroughly at this time.

Looking Forward: Developing a Stress Management Plan

As you end the weekly meetings, shift the emphasis toward preparation in order to maintain progress and gains in coping with stress. To do this, help the patient develop the following:

- A self-monitoring schedule

- A plan for managing automatic thoughts

- A plan for short-term prevention

- A plan for managing bigger stressful life events

- A plan for staying connected with other people

- A booster plan

Each of these items is included in the workbook form titled "My Stress Management Plan." Guide the patient through the following step-by-step instructions to develop this plan:

Step 1: Scheduling Self-Monitoring Check-Ins

Emphasize that self-monitoring is a critical part of an ongoing stress management program. In the past weeks the patient has learned to monitor her thoughts, feelings, and sensations so that she can be aware of the causes of stress and distress in her life. Having a self-monitoring plan is an important part of keeping stress from building or becoming unmanageable.

A self-monitoring plan includes a plan for what to monitor (e.g. signs that stress is increasing) and when to check in. Tell the patient that it is usually best to make an appointment with herself to check in—much as she has done over the past weeks with you—as it is easy to forget to monitor in day-to-day life. Encourage her to schedule this time into her planner. You may want to say the following:

Having a scheduled time to check in with yourself ensures that you will in fact do so. It will provide a structure and a way to bring your attention to bothersome reactions in the past week, identifying ways to handle them, and even setting up an action plan for the following week. It is helpful to schedule a specific time for your weekly check-ins with yourself—perhaps even at the same time as the meetings you have been having. Scheduling the time into your weekly planner can be one way of ensuring that you continue with these regular check-ins.

Weekly Check-Ins

At the end of the workbook is a sheet titled "Weekly Check-In." This is provided as a way of helping patients organize their check-ins. Patients may photocopy the sheet as necessary and record on it the following information:

- Level of stress over the past week

- Any positive things that happened

- How the patient managed the stress

- Any upcoming stressors and how the patient might handle them

- An action plan for the coming week

Early Warning Signs

Knowing our early warning signs is crucial to maintaining our well-being. Emphasize that noticing these may help the patient head off or reduce stressors.

Explain that each person's warning signs will likely be different. Some people may find that they are better at recognizing stress in specific areas of functioning. You may want to say something like the following to illustrate:

> *For example, imagine that four people have the same problem of taking on more and more commitments until they are suddenly overwhelmed. The task for each of them is to identify markers or warning signs that can alert them that they are starting to approach the overwhelmed state before they actually get there. One person may notice that she feels more physically agitated—increased muscle tension, pain—before she becomes overwhelmed. So, for this person, increased agitation, muscle tension, or pain can be used as a sign that a lot of stress and distress is down the road if something isn't changed. Another person may notice that she feels more emotionally anxious. And yet another person might be more tuned into her thinking processes and notice that she is having more negative thoughts. A fourth person may be more aware of changes in her social behavior—how she does less and less with other people and spends more time alone. Certainly everybody has lots of warning signs. But we tend to notice some more than others.*

Have the patient identify the warning signs that tell her when to intervene before her stress level gets even worse. To anticipate these, have the patient think back to recent stressful events and try to remember the main warning signs she experienced that indicated the increasing level of stress. Warning signs may include thoughts, behaviors, emotions, and physical symptoms. Instruct the patient to place the most important warning signs under Step 1 of the My Stress Management Plan in chapter 13 of the workbook and check in on these each week.

Step 2: Managing Unhelpful Thoughts

Over the past weeks the patient has paid attention to the unhelpful thoughts that come up and also ways of countering them. Many people find that certain types of thoughts tend to come up over and over again. Step 2 involves summarizing these. For example, unhelpful thoughts that are common for people who experience a lot of stress are things like "If what I do is not perfect, then I am incompetent," "If I ask for what I want, then people will get angry with me," and so on. Have the patient list some of her most common unhelpful thoughts under Step 2 of the My Stress Management Plan. Also ask her to describe some of the ways she can counter these thoughts.

Step 3: Short-Term Prevention

Big sources of stress are the daily hassles that plague us. These are often recurring annoyances: things like getting stuck in traffic, waiting for appointments longer than one should have to, having friends or colleagues not come through on small promises, and so on. These little things may not have huge consequences, but they are annoying nonetheless. Have the patient list the top strategies that she has found the most helpful in dealing with these kinds of stressors.

Even when we know we should do these things, sometimes it is hard. In the right hand column of Step 3 of the My Stress Management Plan, the patient can put in some of the strategies she has found helpful to get herself to do these things. For example, many people find it hard to do relaxation exercises as consistently or often as they feel would be beneficial. Some people put a relaxation CD they like next to their bed as a reminder to do this exercise before going to sleep.

Step 4: Prepare for the Big Stressors

Some big stressors just happen without warning. But many do give us some warning, like large work assignments or family obligations that might be stressful or conflictual. Explain that to the extent that the patient can anticipate these bigger stressors, she may be able to implement a plan that will at least lessen the impact of these stressors. Under Step 4 of the My Stress Management Plan ask the patient to list in the left hand column the big stressors in her life right now, or those that might be down the road. She can list potential strategies she can use to cope with these stressors in the column on the right.

Step 5: Staying Connected

Emphasize that other people can help—and often they want to. In the left hand column under Step 5 of the My Stress Management Plan have the patient write the names of people who can help her with specific needs. This includes those people who the patient can talk to when she is distressed or upset, people whom she can simply call, people with whom she enjoys spending time, and people who can provide information. There is also a place on the form for the patient to write down what she can do for other people. Remind the patient that doing things for others is often a way of increasing satisfaction and these don't have to be big things (e.g. making a supportive phone call, offering a compliment to a friend, thanking a colleague).

Sometimes people are hesitant to contact others for support. Often this tends to be in a specific area. For example, some people are fine asking for practical support (help doing things) but not very comfortable asking for emotional support (talking with someone when you are distressed). For other people, it may be the other way around. Particularly for those areas or people to whom it is hard to reach out, have the patient list in the right hand column under Step 5 the things she can do to make it easier.

Step 6: Booster Plan

A setback is a recurrence of problems or stress, or a return to unhelpful behaviors, thoughts, or beliefs after a period of improvement or decrease in symptoms. Emphasize that setbacks are a normal part of progress, and, in fact, small to moderate setbacks are useful as potential learning experiences. While these setbacks are perhaps not what the patient wishes for, they provide her with another opportunity to revisit and practice the skills she has learned to manage the difficulty.

Discuss what the patient might do if she finds herself having such a setback. Space for brainstorming is provided under Step 6 of the My Stress Management Plan.

Important Resources

Give the patient a few last tips for maintaining gains:

1. Keep your workbook!

    You have worked very hard to make the changes that you are now experiencing. You now have a written record containing all the notes, exercises, and thoughts regarding your work. Keep this workbook in a place where you can find it easily. It can be a great reference for reviewing tools and a great reminder of your new ability to work through problems.

2. Make use of the last meetings.

    Try working on maintaining your gains over the coming months. Note when there are problems, or what might lead to backsliding. Your coach is still here to assist you.

3. Find substitutes.

    Start thinking about things you can do that will continue to support a good stress management program.

    -   *Are there yoga classes you can attend? Meditation groups?*
    -   *Are there people in your life you can rely on for assistance?*
    -   *Are there ways you can add meaningful activities to your life (regular events like a book club or a class, volunteering in your place of worship, donating time to a political group or a cause you believe in, joining a club or group with similar interests, etc.)?*
    -   *Other ideas?*

Homework

✎ Have the patient finish creating a stress management plan.

✎ Have the patient schedule a time and place for self-monitoring check-ins. The patient should complete a Weekly Check-in sheet.

✎ Have the patient continue to practice one of the relaxation exercises learned during the program.

References

Amato, M. P., Zipoli, V., & Portaccio, E. (2006). Multiple sclerosis-related cognitive changes: A review of cross-sectional and longitudinal studies. *Journal of the Neurological Science, 245*(1–2), 41–46.

Antony, M. M., Brown, T. A., & Barlow, D. H. (1997). Heterogeneity among specific phobia types in DSM-IV. *Behaviour Research and Therapy, 35*(12), 1089–1100.

Beck, J. S. (1995). *Cognitive therapy: Basics and beyond*. New York: Guilford Press.

Beckner, V., Vella, L., Howard, I., & Mohr, D. C. (2007). Alliance in two telephone-administered treatments: Relationship with depression and health outcomes. *Journal of Consulting and Clinical Psychology, 75*(3), 508–512.

Bower, S. A., & Bower, G. H. (1991). *Asserting yourself: A practical guide for positive change*. Reading, MA: Perseus Books.

Burns, D. D. (1999). *Feeling good: The new mood therapy*. New York: Avon Books.

De Jongh, A., Bongaarts, G., Vermeule, I., Visser, K., De Vos, P., & Makkes, P. (1998). Blood-injury-injection phobia and dental phobia. *Behaviour Research and Therapy, 36*, 971–982.

DiMatteo, M. R., Lepper, H. S., & Croghan, T. W. (2000). Depression is a risk factor for noncompliance with medical treatment: Meta-analysis of the effects of anxiety and depression on patient adherence. *Archives of Internal Medicine, 160*, 2101–2107.

Dimidjian, S., Hollon, S. D., Dobson, K. S., Schmaling, K. B., Kohlenberg, R. J., Addis, M. E., et al. (2006). Randomized trial of behavioral activation, cognitive therapy, and antidepressant medication in the acute treatment of adults with major depression. *Journal of Consulting and Clinical Psychology, 74*(4), 658–670.

Edinger, J., & Carney, C. (2008). *Overcoming insomnia: A cognitive-behavioral therapy approach, workbook*. New York: Oxford University Press.

Fisk, J. D., Pontefract, A., Ritvo, P. G., Archibald, C. J., & Murray, T. J. (1994). The impact of fatigue on patients with multiple sclerosis. *Canadian Journal of Neurological Sciences, 21,* 9–14.

Freal, J. E., Kraft, G. H., & Coryell, J. K. (1984). Symptomatic fatigue in multiple sclerosis. *Archives of Physical Medicine and Rehabilitation, 65*(3), 135–138.

Gallagher-Thompson, D., Hanley-Peterson, P., & Thompson, L. W. (1990). Maintenance of gains versus relapse following brief psychotherapy for depression. *Journal of Consulting and Clinical Psychology, 58,* 371–374.

Greenberg, L. S., Rice, L. N., & Elliott, R. (1993). *Facilitating emotional change: The moment-by-moment process.* New York: Guilford Press.

Gronwall, D. (1997). Paced auditory serial-addition task: A measure of recovery from concussion. *Perceptual and Motor Skills, 44,* 367–373.

Hamilton, J. G. (1995). Needle phobia: A neglected diagnosis. *Journal of Family Practice, 41,* 169–175.

Hart, S., Fonareva, I., Merluzzi, N., & Mohr, D. C. (2005). Treatment for depression and its relationship to improvement in quality of life and psychological well-being in multiple sclerosis patients. *Qual Life Research, 14*(3), 695–703.

Hart, S. L., Vella, L., & Mohr, D. C. (2008). Relationships among depressive symptoms, benefit-finding, optimism, and positive affect in multiple sclerosis patients after psychotherapy for depression. *Health Psychology, 27*(2), 230–238.

Hellstrom, K., & Ost, L.-G. (1996). Prediction of outcome in the treatment of specific phobia: A cross-validation study. *Behavioral Research and Therapy, 34*(5/6), 403–411.

Julian, L. J., & Mohr, D. C. (2006). Cognitive predictors of response to treatment for depression in multiple sclerosis. *The Journal of Neuropsychiatry and Clinical Neurosciences, 18*(3), 356–363.

Kazantzis, N., Deane, F. P., & Ronan, K. R. (2000). Homework assignments in cognitive and behavioral therapy: A meta-analysis. *Clinical Psychology: Science and Practice, 7,* 189–202.

Kleinknecht, R. A., Thorndike, R. M., & Walls, M. M. (1996). Factorial dimensions and correlates of blood, injury, injection and related medical fears: Cross validation of the Medical Fear Survey. *Behaviour Research and Therapy, 34*(4), 323–331.

Mohr, D. C., & Cox, D. (2001). Multiple sclerosis: Empirical literature for the clinical health psychologist. *Journal of Clinical Psychology, 57*(4), 479–499.

Mohr, D. C., & Genain, C. (2004). Social support as a buffer in the relationship between treatment for depression and T-cell production of interferon gamma in patients with multiple sclerosis. *Journal of Psychosomatic Research, 57*(2), 155–158.

Mohr, D. C., Boudewyn, A. C., Goodkin, D. E., Bostrom, A., & Epstein, L. (2001). Comparative outcomes for individual cognitive-behavior therapy, supportive-expressive group psychotherapy, and sertraline for the treatment of depression in multiple sclerosis. *Journal of Consulting and Clinical Psychology, 69*(6), 942–949.

Mohr, D. C., Boudewyn, A. C., Likosky, W., Levine, E., & Goodkin, D. E. (2001). Injectable medication for the treatment of multiple sclerosis: The influence of self-efficacy expectations and injection anxiety on adherence and ability to self-inject. *Annals of Behavioral Medicine, 23*(2), 125–132.

Mohr, D. C., Classen, C., & Barrera, M., Jr. (2004). The relationship between social support, depression and treatment for depression in people with multiple sclerosis. *Psychological Medicine, 34*(3), 533–541.

Mohr, D. C., Cox, D., & Merluzzi, N. (2005). Self-injection anxiety training: A treatment for patients unable to self-inject injectable medications. *Multiple Sclerosis, 11*(2), 182–185.

Mohr, D. C., Cox, D., Epstein, L., & Boudewyn, A. (2002). Teaching patients to self-inject: Pilot study of a treatment for injection anxiety and phobia in multiple sclerosis patients prescribed injectable medications. *Journal of Behavior Therapy and Experimental Psychiatry, 33*(1), 39–47.

Mohr, D. C., Epstein, L., Luks, T. L., Goodkin, D., Cox, D., Goldberg, A., et al. (2003). Brain lesion volume and neuropsychological function predict efficacy of treatment for depression in multiple sclerosis. *Journal of Consulting and Clinical Psychology, 71*(6), 1017–1024.

Mohr, D. C., Goodkin, D. E., Bacchetti, P., Boudewyn, A. C., Huang, L., Marrietta, P., et al. (2000). Psychological stress and the subsequent appearance of new brain MRI lesions in MS. *Neurology, 55*(1), 55–61.

Mohr, D. C., Goodkin, D. E., Likosky, W., Gatto, N., Baumann, K. A., & Rudick, R. A. (1997). Treatment of depression improves adherence to interferon beta-1b therapy for multiple sclerosis. *Archives of Neurology, 54*(5), 531–533.

Mohr, D. C., Goodkin, D. E., Likosky, W., Gatto, N., Neilley, L. K., Griffen, C., et al. (1996). Therapeutic expectations of patients with multiple sclerosis upon initiating interferon beta-1b: Relationship to adherence to treatment. *Multiple Sclerosis, 2,* 222–226.

Mohr, D. C., Hart, S. L., Fonareva, I., & Tasch, E. S. (2006). Treatment of depression for patients with multiple sclerosis in neurology clinics. *Multiple Sclerosis, 12*(2), 204–208.

Mohr, D. C., Hart, S. L., & Goldberg, A. (2003). Effects of treatment for depression on fatigue in multiple sclerosis. *Psychosomatic Medicine, 65*(4), 542–547.

Mohr, D. C., Hart, S. L., Howard, I., Julian, L., Vella, L., Catledge, C., et al. (2006). Barriers to psychotherapy among depressed and non-depressed primary care patients. *Annals of Behavioral Medicine, 32*(3), 254–258.

Mohr, D. C., Hart, S. L., Julian, L., Catledge, C., Honos-Webb, L., Vella, L., et al. (2005). Telephone-administered psychotherapy for depression. *Archives of General Psychiatry, 62*(9), 1007–1014.

Mohr, D. C., Hart, S. L., Julian, L., Cox, D., & Pelletier, D. (2004). Association between stressful life events and exacerbation in multiple sclerosis: A meta-analysis. *British Medical Journal, 328*(7442), 731.

Mohr, D. C., Hart, S. L., & Marmar, C. M. (2006). Telephone-administered cognitive-behavioral therapy for the treatment of depression in a rural primary care clinic. *Cognitive Therapy and Research, 30*, 29–37.

Mohr, D. C., Hart, S., & Vella, L. (2007). Reduction in disability in a randomized controlled trial of telephone-administered cognitive-behavioral therapy. *Health Psychology, 26*(5), 554–563.

Mohr, D. C., Likosky, W., Bertagnolli, A., Goodkin, D. E., Van Der Wende, J., Dwyer, P., et al. (2000). Telephone-administered cognitive-behavioral therapy for the treatment of depressive symptoms in multiple sclerosis. *Journal of Consulting and Clinical Psychology, 68*(2), 356–361.

Mohr, D. C., Shoham-Salomon, V., Engle, D., & Beutler, L. E. (1991). The expression of anger in psychotherapy: Its role and measurement. *Psychotherapy Research, 1*, 124–134.

Mohr, D. C., Vella, L., Hart, S., Heckman, T., & Simon, G. (2008). The effect of telephone-administered psychotherapy on symptoms of depression and attrition: A meta-analysis. *Clinical Psychology: Science and Practice, 15*(3), 243–253.

Mollema, E., Snoek, F., Ader, H. J., Heine, R., & van der Ploeg, H. (2001). Insulin-treated diabetes patients with fear of self-injecting or fear of self-testing: Psychological comorbidity and general well-being. *Journal of Psychosomatic Research, 51*, 665–672.

Noseworthy, J. H., Lucchinetti, C., Rodriguez, M., & Weinshenker, B. G. (2000). Multiple sclerosis. *The New England Journal of Medicine*, *343*(13), 938–952.

O'Connor, A. B., Schwid, S. R., Herrmann, D. N., Markman, J. D., & Dworkin, R. H. (2008). Pain associated with multiple sclerosis: Systematic review and proposed classification. *Pain, 137*(1), 96–111.

Patten, S. B., Beck, C. A., Williams, J. V., Barbui, C., & Metz, L. M. (2003). Major depression in multiple sclerosis: A population-based perspective. *Neurology, 61*(11), 1524–1527.

Pollin, I. (1995). *Medical crisis counseling: Short-term therapy for long-term illness.* New York: Norton.

Sadovnick, A. D., Remick, R. A., Allen, J., Swartz, E., Yee, I. M., Eisen, K., et al. (1996). Depression and multiple sclerosis. *Neurology, 46*(3), 628–632.

Schwartz, C. E., & Sendor, R. M. (1999). Helping others helps oneself: Response shift effects in peer support. *Social Science and Medicine, 48*, 1563–1575.

Siegert, R. J., & Abernethy, D. A. (2005). Depression in multiple sclerosis: A review. *Journal of Neurology, Neurosurgery Psychiatry, 76*(4), 469–475.

Spiegel, D., & Classen, C. (2000). *Group therapy for cancer patients: A research-based handbook of psychosocial care.* New York: Basic Books.

Thompson, L. W., Gallagher, D., Breckenridge, J. S. (1987). Comparative effectiveness of psychotherapies for depressed elders. *Journal of Consulting and Clinical Psychology, 55*, 385–390.

Uchino, B. N. (2004). *Social support and physical health: Understanding the health consequences of relationships.* New Haven, CT: Yale University Press.

Watson, J. C., Gordon, L. B., Stermac, L., Kalogerakos, F., & Steckley, P. (2003). Comparing the effectiveness of process-experiential with cognitive-behavioral psychotherapy in the treatment of depression. *Journal of Consulting and Clinical Psychology, 71*(4), 773–781.

About the Author

David C. Mohr, PhD, is a clinical psychologist and Professor in the Department of Preventive Medicine at Northwestern University. He received his doctorate at the University of Arizona in 1991, and began his career on the faculty of the University of California, San Francisco, in the Department of Neurology's Multiple Sclerosis (MS) Center.

Dr. Mohr is an active researcher who has studied the treatment of depression in people with MS and developed a behavioral intervention to treat injection anxiety. He has also conducted several studies examining the relationship between stress and MS disease activity. More recently he has begun developing and evaluating Technology-Assisted Psychological Interventions, including the use of the Internet and mobile phones to deliver treatment. Dr. Mohr's research has been funded by the National Institutes of Health as well as the National MS Society. He has published over 80 scientific papers in peer-reviewed journals, has contributed numerous chapters to edited books, and has worked on several guidelines for the treatment of MS. Dr. Mohr is a Fellow of the Academy of Behavioral Medicine Research, and of the Society of Behavioral Medicine.